# Leadership Paradigms in Chaplaincy

## Joel Curtis Graves

**DISSERTATION.COM**

Boca Raton

*Leadership Paradigms in Chaplaincy*

Dissertation.com
Boca Raton, Florida
USA • 2007

ISBN: 1-58112- 372-8
13-ISBN: 978-1-58112-372-2

ETHICS STATEMENT

I am the sole author of the content and ideas set forth in this study, except where I

acknowledge other authors and contributors through citations and quotations.

TABLE OF CONTENTS

# ACKNOWLEDGEMENTS

I wish to thank and bless the Lord Jesus Christ for the work of the Holy Spirit in my life, which has prompted me to work in the area of chaplaincy and has sustained me through the vagaries of life. My wife, Rena, the love of my life, and kids, Joshua and Christina, support and bless me every day. My parents, Curtis and Patsy Graves, set the example early in my life, for a life well-lived in God's service. The President of Faith Evangelical Lutheran Seminary, Tacoma, Washington, Dr. Michael Adams' support and mentorship throughout my theological education and beyond have been a magnificent blessing. He had a vision of me in ministry from the minute I walked into his office. Dr. James Gibson and Dr. Gary Waldron are gifted teachers and men of faith, whose training, expertise, and passion for ministry have inspired me long after the classes were over. Dr. Gordon Hilsman and Rev. Dr. Arthur Schmidt, my Clinical Pastoral Education supervisors at St. Joseph Medical Center, Tacoma, mentored me through ministry formation and helped me find my ministry, my voice, and my self. There were many others: peers, coworkers, patients, and staff: Thank you and bless you all.

# CHAPTER 1

## STATEMENT OF PROBLEM

Traditionally, chaplains don't tend to draw attention to themselves as they quietly go about their business. But the needs of people are growing and society is changing. I say *the needs of people are growing* because of the growing gap between the have's and the have not's, more people outside the church than in (many unchurched or dechurched), a growing discontent and violence in the world evidenced by school shootings and terrorism, generalized fears and angers, and the many people who seem to have a spiritual thirst for something they can't even identify.

In chaplaincy and in many churches, leadership, management, and ministry have a synergistic effect when they come together in response to a problem or crisis. An understanding of chaplaincy dynamics, scope, methods, possibilities, and issues in relation to this effect is vital to this growing field in four areas: (1) It helps prepare people for ministry as chaplains, whether clergy or lay; (2) It benefits those already in chaplaincy ministry; (3) It helps clergy reexamine their ministry to determine if they are where God wants them; and, (4) It serves to teach everyone, including upper-level management and senior church leaders (first-chair leaders), of the roles, actual or potential, that chaplains can fill in response to the growing needs of people.

If chaplaincy is to be effective across a broad spectrum of ministry and in the great diversity of settings, it is important to standardize training overall, and if appropriate, train chaplains in the area of management. This will be a giant step in this growing field and increase the professionalism of the group as a whole. Success in ministry and the quality of ministry do not happen by accident; they are the purposeful result of a response to a divine calling, coupled with sincere effort, effective training, respect for people, and skillful execution.

## IMPORTANCE OF THE PROBLEM

Chaplains are leaders, and they must be at the forefront of ministry to people on the fringes of our churches and society. Without chaplains helping to meet the growing needs of these people, we will not be fulfilling the mandate to take the Gospel into the whole world, addressing the justice needs of people, or helping alleviate suffering. Simply put, we might finally reach the unreached peoples groups of foreign countries and fail in our mission to reach the people at home.

Chaplain leadership can be enigmatic. The leadership dynamics and concepts in the ministry of chaplains flow from different sources and perspectives, then are articulated in a variety of ways which do not necessarily fit with the standard literature on leadership. Yet, leadership concepts applicable to chaplains can be found in all leadership studies, in their various forms and possibilities. Chaplains are ministers and leaders outside the traditional church building to people who need clergy support, and they often exert great influence on the people they encounter. Although some chaplaincy organizations have continued to challenge their members to grow in training and professionalism, this is not true everywhere. In many areas, people are answering the call to chaplaincy, but are having to learn on the job, through trial and error, and their effectiveness, success, and quality are very elusive or spotty at best. This study addresses

2

some of the areas necessary for successful chaplaincy, although each ministry is unique and has its own challenges.

In this study, I want to look at the history of chaplains and the associated leadership perspectives; look briefly at different types of chaplaincies; discuss contemporary church leadership, chaplain management and leadership dynamics; then look at the work of chaplains, some of their tools, and associated leadership issues.

## THESIS

Clergy, lay persons, business people, and many chaplains do not understand the leadership and management dynamics of chaplaincy, and this lack of knowledge has a direct impact on how chaplaincy is done and not done in certain areas. In chaplaincy and many churches, leadership, management, and ministry have a synergistic effect when they come together in response to a problem or crisis. An understanding of chaplaincy dynamics, scope, methods, possibilities, and issues in relation to this effect is vital to this growing field in four areas: Helps prepare people for ministry as chaplains, whether clergy or lay; benefits those already in chaplaincy ministry; helps clergy reexamine their ministry to determine if they are where God wants them; serves to teach everyone, including upper-level management and senior church leaders of the roles, actual or potential, that chaplains can fill in response to the growing needs of people.

## DEFINITION OF MAJOR TERMS

### Chaplain

A chaplain is a person (clergy or lay) who represents a religious and/or spiritual perspective in an institution or organization, and who ministers to people in need. In some places, the chaplain may not be clergy, while in other places like many hospitals, there are numerous requirements, including specialized education, training, and certification.

### Chaplaincy

Chaplaincy is the location and work of the chaplain, in whatever place that might take them, in a variety of settings. A person might say, "I am in the chaplaincy," the way someone might say, "I am in the pastorate." It is a way of saying that someone is served or ministry takes place. The work of the chaplaincy is whatever the chaplain does to help those in need. It can be as simple as listening or as dangerous as accompanying soldiers on patrol.

### Clinical Pastoral Education (CPE)

From 1920 to 1922, the Reverend Anton Boisen was hospitalized for schizophrenia. Based on his experience in the mental institution, he believed that certain types of schizophrenia were problems of the soul. In 1925, Dr. William A. Bryan, Superintendent of Worcestor State Hospital, Worcester, Massachusetts, hired Rev. Boisen as a hospital chaplain. In an attempt to study the relationship between religion and medicine, Chaplain Boisen invited four students to work with him in the hospital. At the same time, Dr. Richard C. Cabot suggested that theological students at Harvard Divinity School do an internship in the medical school. Boisen endorsed this program and clinical ministry began.[1]

In the last eighty years, CPE has become an international organization that trains people in a variety of clinical settings. Usually in a hospital, a trained and certified supervisor directs a group of four to eight students at a time who perform ministry in different parts of the facility, including satellite or branch operations (hospice, soup kitchens, skilled nursing facilities, mental institutions, dialysis clinics, etc.).

There are two programs: regular and extended. The regular program is on a quarterly schedule and has two types of students: residents and interns. The interns are in a non-paid position and can work in different units (also known as *wards*) each quarter (rehabilitation, mental health, oncology, renal dialysis, etc.). The residents are in paid positions for one year, usually specializing in one particular area (one of the branches or a hospital unit). The extended program is for students who can only attend part-time and usually meet once or twice a week in the evening with a supervisor and the group. They are assigned to a hospital unit or branch, where they work part-time for their ministry experience. They earn one point of credit for approximately eight months of work, which equates to one point a year. There are extended groups which earn two credits per year.

To successfully complete a CPE course and meet the minimum requirements for most hospital employment opportunities and certification, a student must earn four credits, which equates to four quarters of training.

The regular CPE training environment consists of two five hour weekly supervised peer group meetings, a one hour weekly supervisor meeting, verbatims of

---

[1] Joan E. Hemenway, *Inside the Circle: A historical and practical inquiry concerning process groups in clinical pastoral education.* (Decatur, GA: Journal of Pastoral Care Publications), 1996.

chaplain/other person (patient, client, family, staff) interactions that are discussed in the group, programmed training/classes, book reviews, and diverse didactics with guest speakers. The students are immersed in ministry and report to their peer group and supervisor on what happens in that ministry, how the patient reacts, how they react, and especially how they feel. It is important to determine what goes on actually but also personally, as they learn who they are and often validate their call to ministry of any kind.

Who takes CPE? Many seminaries require at least one quarter of CPE, which seminarians often complete during a summer break. Some people feel called to a clinical ministry and explore that calling by taking CPE. Then there are others who just want the experience and training to learn how to serve people in great need and suffering, as in a church visitation ministry.

## Disenfranchised Grief

Loss is a fact of human existence as is the resultant grief that follows. People have a right to grieve their losses. But when a person who needs to grieve and cannot because of complications from relationships, societal restrictions, and a variety of other problems, that grief is said to be disenfranchised. Dr. Doka, who first coined the term *disenfranchised grief* in relation to people who experienced a problem with loss and grief, wrote, "The loss cannot be openly acknowledged, socially validated, or publicly mourned."[2] In another place he wrote, "The person experiences a loss, but the resulting grief is unrecognized by others. The person has no socially accorded right to grieve that loss or to mourn it in that particular way. The grief is disenfranchised."[3]

---

[2] Kenneth J. Doka, ed., *Disenfranchised Grief: new directions, challenges, and strategies for practice* (Champaign, Ill.: Research Press, 2002), xiii.
[3] Doka, *Disenfranchised Grief*, 7.

For example, sometimes children are not allowed to attend a family funeral, or their grief is not acknowledged as important. They carry the burden of the loss in themselves, and it often gets expressed as acting out, behavioral changes, bed wetting, fighting among siblings, and poor school performance. In another example, parents might not attend the funeral of their grown child who committed suicide or died in prison. Chaplains often run into people suffering from complicated grief issues like these, and unresolved grief can affect a person's emotional and physical health, and hinder healing.

First Chair

The concept of *first chair* refers to the person who is the head of an organization, the leader and person in charge, who makes the final decisions. In a church, this is usually the senior pastor.

Influence

*Influence* means having the ability to produce a response in a person and affect their thoughts or actions.[4] In the realm of leadership, influence is said to be the basis of leadership.[5] In this way, influence is how we relate to the people around us. We cause influence, and we experience the influence of others: influence goes out from one person to another and requires a response. Influence can grow and wane based on the personality and character of the leader.

---

[4] Oxford American Dictionary-Heald Colleges Edition, "Influence," (New York: Avon Books, 1982), 454.
[5] John C. Maxwell, *Developing the Leader Within You* (Nashville: Thomas Nelson, 1993), 1.

JCAHO

Pronounced *jay-co*, the Joint Commission on the Accreditation of Healthcare

Organizations, is also known as the Joint Commission. The American College of

Surgeons (ACS) began inspecting volunteer hospitals in 1917 to raise the standard of

healthcare. Using the idea of *end result system of hospital standardization*, a hospital

would follow up on patients who had been treated to determine if the treatment was

effective. If it was not, the hospital was supposed to determine why and try to correct the

problem for the benefit of future patients. In 1951, the ACS was joined by the American

Medical Association,, the American College of Physicians, the American Hospital

Association, and the Canadian Medical Association to form the Joint Commission on

Accreditation of Hospitals.

In 1965, Congress passed an amendment to Social Security stating that hospitals

must be in compliance with Medicare Conditions of Participation to participate and get

paid for Medicare and Medicaid programs. The money from these programs is important

to a healthcare organization's profitability. Determining compliance with this law and

accrediting hospitals who comply with the provisions is the job of the Joint Commission.

Today, the Joint Commission evaluates and accredits approximately 15,000 healthcare

organizations and programs, and its mission is to "continuously improve the safety and

quality of care provided to the public through the provision of health care accreditation

and related services that support performance improvement in health care

organizations."[6]

---

[6] Joint Commission on the Accreditation of Healthcare Organizations, "About Us," Oct 2006, *JCAHO Web*, http://www.jointcommission.org/AboutUs/joint_commission_facts.htm (28 Oct 2006).

JCAHO requires that a spiritual assessment be done to determine if there are spiritual issues related to the patient's healthcare. The established standard not only requires a definition of the spiritual assessment, but also the qualifications of the people performing the assessment. In that regard, the criteria for chaplains has grown to ensure the highest quality patient care, and chaplains must now be board certified by recognized certification agencies, like the Association of Professional Chaplains, the National Association of Catholic Chaplains, or the National Association of Jewish Chaplains. The section on Healthcare Chaplains has more detail about certification.

Leadership

To *lead* means to influence the actions or opinions of another.[7] The person who has the lead causes leadership when the effect of influence happens to people: cause and effect. John Maxwell wrote that leadership is influence."[8] Leadership implies followers. In the church, the designated first chair person exercises leadership over a group of people willing to subject themselves to that person's influence. The inverse would also be true, that the loss of influence means that a person has lost the ability to lead the group, and the leadership is less effective or a failure.

Medical Ethics

Medical ethics is also known by the names *Clinical Ethics*, *Biomedical Ethics*, *Healthcare Ethics*, and *Bioethics*. Medical ethics is about the moral principles of patient autonomy, beneficence, nonmaleficence, and justice. In many medical cases, there is a sense of urgency, and the medical ethical dilemma must be resolved quickly and a

---

[7] Dictionary, "Lead," 503.
[8] Maxwell, *Developing the Leader*, 1.

decision made. In the section on the Jonseniand Paradigm, medical ethics principles and a technique for determining a course of action are covered in more detail.

The Jonseniand Paradigm is useful for people working in healthcare, but also for ministers who get involved in the healthcare issues of their church members. Issues of quality versus quantity of life often come up. For example, a church member wants to talk to the pastor about stopping the cancer treatments and wants advice based on shared beliefs. Another church member has a husband who wrote in his living will, that he did not want to live in a persistent vegetative state when his Parkinson's disease got real bad. After three years of steadily declining health, she now wants to honor his wishes and wants to know what her pastor thinks about stopping his tube feedings and letting him die.

Palliative Care

The simplest definition of palliative care is *comfort care*. Palliative care is a key component of hospice care, because a patient's relief from emotional, physical, and spiritual pain is a primary goal in helping them die in peace. Palliative care services include symptom control,  pain control, counseling, religious and spiritual ministry, music therapy, massage and various healing touch therapies, and various support systems. Palliative care is a team approach with doctors, nurses, social workers, chaplains, bereavement counselors, bath aides, and volunteers all working together to improve and maintain a high quality of life at the patient's end of life. This care affirms life and neither hastens nor postpones death.

Pastoral Authority

Jesus presented and represented the idea of a spiritual leader being a shepherd of people. "I am the good shepherd; I know my sheep and my sheep know me."[9] *Pastor* means shepherd and *pastoral* relates to the duties of the pastor. The pastor shepherds people the way a shepherd in the field takes care of a flock of sheep. Pastoral authority is the shepherd's authority over the flock in their charge, as a part of their duties. In the church, pastoral authority is about the expectation people have in a religious or spiritual leader to exercise influence over them based on history, culture, and experience. The position of authority comes from a denomination, organization, or congregation, and is often called ordination. In this position, the ordained person is expected to carry out certain agreed upon teachings, rituals, sacraments, and celebrations in a recognized format.

Second Chair

The concept of *second chair* refers to the person who works with and for the first chair person who is in charge, subordinate to the first chair leader. In a church, this could be the executive pastor, assistant pastor, youth minister, or a ministry leader.

Servanthood

"Whoever wants to become great among you must be your servant, and whoever wants to be the first must be the slave of all."[10] In this statement, Jesus is speaking about the attitude that he wants his followers to have in the Church. "You know that those who are regarded as rulers of the Gentiles lord it over them, and their high officials exercise

---

[9] John 10:14.
[10] Mark 10:43-44.

authority over them. Not so with you."[11] The Gentile-style or worldly type of leadership would be the opposite of servanthood, as defined by Jesus. In the Church, leaders should have a servanthood attitude in their relationships to fulfill these scriptures.

Spirituality

I define spirituality as the upward, inward, and outward aspects of a relationship and connection to something other than our selves. *Other* is anything higher or greater or deeper than our personal self, such as transcendence, immanence, and life's mysteries, which brings fulfillment. Transcendence means *going beyond*, and immanence is considered the opposite of transcendence and means *to remain within or contained within*.[12] In Christianity God is transcendent and at the same time is immanent in the incarnation.[13]

Spiritual Assessment

Spiritual assessment is the purposeful determination of the patient's support systems, coping abilities, and relationships with a higher power, themselves, and others with the goal of helping or assisting them with spiritual issues and problems. There are different spiritual assessment models and many different questions that can be asked to find what concerns a person in relation to their spiritual needs.

Spiritual Leadership

Spiritual leadership is influence on the spiritual level, which includes issues of transcendence, connections, meaning, contentment, relationships, support, grief, loss,

[11] Matt 20:25.
[12] Wikipedia Encyclopedia, "Transcendence," http://en.wikipedia.org/wiki/Transcendence_(philosophy) (30 Nov 2006).
[13] Wikipedia Encyclopedia, "Immanence," http://en.wikipedia.org/wiki/Immanence (30 Nov 2006).

hope, coping, values, ethics, sacred tradition, sacraments, music, ritual, presence, beliefs, prayer, meditation, reconciliation, and end of life.

All people have spiritual needs, which change over time and circumstances. The person with spiritual leadership ministers to people with spiritual needs. People in hospitals have strong spiritual needs, and chaplains are in a unique position to minister to them.

Theological Reflection

As the name implies, theological reflection is reflecting on an experience or situation theologically, usually using the Bible. Theological reflection takes place in the space where experience and the scriptures meet. It asks the question, "What does God have to say in this situation?" God speaks to us through direct revelation, the scriptures of the Bible, and the wise counsel of those people we respect and hear. Theological reflection can be used to minister to ourselves and others. I believe theological reflection is a way the Holy Spirit speaks to us, and helps a person understand their ministry better and grow spiritually.

Unchurched and Dechurched

George Barna was the first to coin the term, *Unchurched*, in a study his group conducted on church attendance and beliefs in the United States. The Barna Group define unchurched as, "an adult (18 or older) who has not attended a Christian church service within the past six months, not including a holiday service (such as Easter or Christmas) or a special event at a church (such as a wedding or funeral)."[14]

---

[14] George Barna, "Unchurched," *The Barna Group Web*. http://www.barna.org/FlexPage.aspx?Page=Topic&TopicID=38 (12 Nov 2006).

I disagree with the Barna definition. To me, *unchurched* means someone has had no church exposure. People who were in church at one time, perhaps when young, but do not attend anymore for a myriad of reasons are more accurately described as *dechurched.* Although they might consider themselves Christians or believers, they either got out of the habit of going, were somehow disenfranchised by formal religion, or just felt it was no longer important. Like the unchurched, many claim to have a form of spirituality that is intimately personal and meets their needs, or they believe nothing and don't feel compelled to believe anything, as long as life is cruising along without troubles.

In many cases, the formal church has had little impact in their lives, as an entity or through an individual. Many of the dechurched do not have a Christian belief system anymore, but they might say they have a form of spirituality, which they claim meets their needs for inner contentment.

In both groups, the religious ideas and concepts of sin, heaven, hell, Jesus, God, and Satan are often rejected or just ignored. Some people can carry their personal spirituality into all phases of their lives with little conflict, but for some it fails in a personal crisis. When these people experience great need and suffering, such as in illness or loss, Chaplains must move through this area of personal spirituality with great sensitivity and respect, if they are going to help.

Unreached Peoples Groups

Ethnic groups of people living in foreign countries who have not heard or read the Gospel are considered unreached. For two thousand years, Christian church groups and individuals have taken the Gospel into the farthest reaches to fulfill the mandate from

Jesus Christ to take the Gospel into all the world.[15]

## HISTORICAL ANTECEDENTS

I am not aware of previous work done in the area of chaplaincy leadership and

management dynamics.

## SCOPE AND LIMITATIONS OF THIS PROJECT

Although the scope of this study was to look at chaplain leadership patterns and

examples, it was possible that some people reading this might want to know more about

what a chaplain is and what chaplains do. In that light, I expanded the study a little to

give the best possible overview while supporting the original intent.

## METHODOLOGY

This dissertation is an historical and exegetical analysis of chaplaincy in history with

attention to leadership dimensions and traits, and analysis of leadership concepts relevant

to ministry, business, and management as applied to chaplaincy.

---

[15] Acts 1:8.

## CHAPTER OUTLINE

Chapter 2 of this study describes chaplaincy from its earliest beginnings in history and takes the reader through the development of chaplaincy, including leadership dynamics in all its forms to the present day.

Chapter 3 describes the different religions in chaplaincy and types of chaplaincies in an effort to show the depth of the ministry in all its facets.

Chapter 4 looks at leadership in relation to church ministry, chaplaincy, women in leadership, and talks about the concepts of authority, influence, and servanthood.

Chapter 5 is about the chaplain as leader and manager and how these aspects differ in chaplaincy leadership. It discusses the leadership requirements in churches and chaplaincies, the difference between leadership and management, and a discussion of the skills required for the chaplain leader manager role.

Chapter 6 looks at the First Chair leadership concept, a theology of pastoral care, ethics, and tolerance in an effort to show some of the leadership dynamics and challenges in chaplaincy.

Chapter 7 carries forward the theme from the previous chapter but talks more about how things are done and how ministry takes place. Spiritual assessment, self-care, theological reflection, and disenfranchised grief are important issues in chaplaincy ministry and affect leadership and management dynamics.

Chapter 8 summarizes the previous work and has more of my own personal reflections on the subject.

# CHAPTER 2 – CHAPLAINCY IN HISTORY AND AMERICA

Throughout history, military organizations and religious establishments have been closely linked. The crisis of war caused people to seek their gods for divine guidance, protection, and victory on the battlefields. When attacked, the military and religious leaders quickly came together to defeat the threat to their lives and way of life. At different times the religious leaders played a key and pivotal role, and at other times a supporting role.

The problems and tensions of war and faith, and the morality of war, have always been present.

> Throughout the long history of Christianity, three major stances on this dreadful subject [of war] have prevailed: the crusader, the pacifist, and the combatant who participates in war as a grim reality and sad necessity of life while wishing wholeheartedly for peace, good will toward men. Many, if not most chaplains, went to war though longing for peace and the quiet life of their homes, churches, and communities.[16]

Whatever the cause and no matter how they felt about it, many clergy and religious leaders felt compelled by God to lead or follow their congregations, the people of their charge, to war and into battle. Some ministers, men and women, did not enter combat, but saw the crisis of war as an opportunity for spreading the gospel, both by their good works and their words, to their own soldiers, the enemy, and non-combatants on the fringe.

---

[16] Parker C. Thompson, *From Its European Antecedents to 1791: The United States Army Chaplaincy* (6 vols.; Washington DC: Office of the Chief of Chaplains, Department of the Army, 1978), 1:95.

## THE LEGEND OF MARTIN OF TOURS

According to legend, Martin of Tours was a Roman soldier who gave his cloak to a
shivering beggar. That night he dreamed that Christ was wearing his cloak, so he became
a Christian and devoted himself to service in the church. When he died, his cloak became
a holy relic and was kept in a little shrine called the *capella*. Frankish kings carried the
cloak into battle believing it would give them victory. The priests in charge of the cloak
and the shrine for these fighting kings were called the *capellani*, and went anywhere the
army traveled. In time all clergy in the military were called by this name, which became
*chapelain* in French and then the familiar *chaplain*.[17]


## CHAPLAINCY IN THE BIBLE

Probably the oldest known relationship between the military and religion in all of history
comes from Genesis. In Genesis 14, there was a war. Led by Kedorlaomer, the four kings
of the cities Shinar, Ellasar, Elam, and Goiim attacked the five kings of the cities Sodom,
Gomorrah, Admah, Zeboiim, and Zoar. The five cities were ransacked, and goods,
livestock, and people were carried off, including Abram's nephew, Lot, who lived in
Sodom. Abram had three hundred and eighteen fighting men born in his household, and
late that night he attacked the four kings, routed and drove them north, took back all of
the plunder, and rescued Lot and his family.

Verse 18 says, "Then Melchizedek king of Salem brought out bread and wine. He
was a priest of God Most High, and he blessed Abram, saying, 'Blessed be Abram by

---

[17] Earl F. Stover, *Up From Handymen: The United States Army Chaplaincy 1865-1920* (6 vols.; Honolulu:
University Press of the Pacific, 2004), 3:235.

God Most High, Creator of heaven and earth. And blessed be God Most High, who delivered your enemies into your hand.' Then Abram gave him a tenth of everything."

Melchizedek blesses Abram in the name of God Most High. There was probably a ritual ceremony with the bread and wine, perhaps a type of communion, and he comes from a town that would become better known as Jerusalem – the City of Peace. Melchizedek reminds Abram that it was God who gave him the victory. It is notable that Abram acts like he is expecting Melchizedek, and it is obvious that he respects him and his authority, because he does not argue with the tithe. The Bible does not mention that Melchizedek asked for the tithe; Abram just gave it, so it probably was an established custom of the times for those people who shared a common belief in God Most High.

God told Moses that priests were necessary for a successful outcome in all battles by reminding the people who were fighting, that it was God who gave the victory:

> When you are about to go into battle, the priest shall come forward and address the army. He shall say: "Hear, O Israel, today you are going into battle against your enemies. Do not be fainthearted or afraid; do not be terrified or give way to panic before them. For the Lord your God is the one who goes with you to fight for you against your enemies to give you the victory."[18]

Priests accompanied the military on their campaigns and into battle as far back as Joshua (1400 B.C.E.) and were given key roles to play in defeating the enemy.

> Then the Lord said to Joshua, "See, I have delivered Jericho into your hands, along with its king and its fighting men. March around the city once with all the armed men. Do this for six days. Have seven priests carry trumpets of rams' horns in front of the ark. On the seventh day, march around the city seven times, with the priests blowing the trumpets. When you hear them sound a long blast on the trumpets, have all the people give a loud shout; then the wall of the city will collapse and the people will go up, every man straight in."[19]

---

[18]Deut 20:2-4, *New International Version.*
[19] Josh 6:2-5.

In the book of Numbers, Balak the King of Moab, hired the sorcerer and prophet, Balaam, to bring a curse down on the Israelites. "A people has come out of Egypt; they cover the face of the land and have settled next to me. Now come and put a curse on these people, because they are too powerful for me. Perhaps then I will be able to defeat them and drive them out of the country. For I know that those you bless are blessed, and those you curse are cursed."[20] In this story, Balaam keeps blessing Israel instead of cursing them until Balak finally fires him.


## ARMED AND DANGEROUS

In 742, the Council of Ratisbon authorized Catholic priests to accompany armies but not to carry weapons or fight.[21] But in 1066, William the Conqueror's half-brother, Bishop Odo, fought alongside his brother with a heavy blunt mace (he had sworn an oath not to use sharp-edged weapons).

Chaplains have a long and storied history in England, and the present day work of chaplains was greatly influenced by these early clergy. In the 1500's, the Tudors instituted the regimental chaplain system, stating that the regimental commander should have "a well-governed and religious preacher in his regiment so that by this life and doctrines the soldiers may be drawn to goodness."[22]

St. John Capistrano is the patron saint of chaplains. John was born in Capistrano, Italy in 1385 and became governor of Perugia. When war broke out between Perugia and neighboring Malatesta in 1416, he was sent by the King of Naples to broker piece. The Malatestians threw him in prison, where he had a vision of St. Francis, who told him to

---

[20] Num 22:5b-6.
[21] Thompson, *European Antecedents*, 1:xi.
[22] Thompson, *European Antecedents*, 1:xii-xiii.

join the Franciscan order. Upon his release from prison, he joined the Franciscans and became famous for his preaching and piety. As an inquisitor, he defended the Catholic faith but was very hard on Jews, Hussites, Fraticellis, and Jesuatis. In 1456, as the Hungarians fought the Ottomans, John Capistrano, now 70 years old, successfully led the left flank of the army at the Battle of Belgrade. He died two years later and was canonized in 1690. (Because the records of that time are uncertain, the date of canonization has also been set at 1724).[23]

Spanish explorers were accompanied by Catholic priests on their expeditions, who looked after the men and spread the gospel to the peoples encountered. Franciscan, Frey Juan de Padilla, traveled with Coronado in search of the fabled *Eldorado*, the city of gold; traveling up from Mexico into what is now the central United States. When the expedition turned back, Father Padilla stayed behind with a few others to share the gospel with the local Indians. One day, they came across a band of Indians who appeared hostile, but Father Padilla was not alarmed. He told his companions to hide in the tall prairie grass and went out, unarmed, to meet them. He was filled with arrows on the plains of southwest Kansas in 1542. Another chaplain, years later, would write: "Chaplain Padilla set a standard in America for loyalty to his mission and love for his friends and foes alike."[24]

The first chaplain in America was the Reverend Robert Hunt. He was appointed chaplain for the purpose of accompanying the merchants in establishing the colony of Jamestown in 1607. As an Anglican, he held services each morning and evening, preached two sermons on Sundays, and gave communion once every three months. He

---

[23] Catholic Encyclopedia, "St. John Capistran," *Catholic Encyclopedia Web.*
http://www.newadvent.org/cathen/08452.htm (30 Oct 2006).
[24] Thompson, *European Antecedents*, 1:2.

was noted for his patience, godly exhortations, and devout example. He was instrumental in keeping the peace among the colonists and encouraging a united front in light of their considerable difficulties with weather, Indians, and starvation. He suffered from poor health, and although we don't know how he died, he apparently died in 1608. "Captain Smith wrote: 'Master Robert Hunt, an honest, religious and couragious Divine; during whose life our factions were oft qualified, our wants and greatest extremities so comforted, that they seemed easie in comparison of what we endured after his memorable death.' "[25]

The Reverend Samuel Stone was the first military chaplain in America. The Pequot Indians declared war on the colonists of Connecticut in 1637. In March, they attacked Fort Saybrook, and in April, the town of Weathersfield, killing two people and capturing two girls. Captain John Mason organized a force to rescue the girls, but there was controversy over what military action to take, and the townspeople rejected Captain Mason's plan.

In a moment of extraordinary faith, Captain Mason turned to Chaplain Stone and asked him to pray to God for divine guidance as to which course of action would bring victory. Chaplain Stone retired to their ship and spent the rest of the day and night praying and waiting on the Lord. The next morning, he went ashore and announced that God wanted them to follow Captain Mason's plan.

Following Mason's plan, they sailed north up the coast past the Pequot villages to the Thames River and went ashore. This maneuver would allow them to come upon the Pequots from behind. In this endeavor, they were able to enlist the aid of the Pequot's old

---

[25] Thompson, *European Antecedents*, 1:6.

enemies, the Miantonomohs. The following morning, their predawn attack on the Pequots was a complete surprise, and the Pequot Nation was utterly destroyed.[26]

During the time of the French and Indian wars in America, thirty-one clergy served as local militia and chaplains and took their congregations into battle. A record of that fighting stated that the chaplains were from the Congregationalist, Presbyterian, and Episcopal churches.

## CLERGY IN UNIFORM – TWO ULTIMATE AUTHORITIES

Clergy represent God, and as such, are accountable to God for all of their words and actions. Clergy in the employ of the military, chaplains, are also accountable to their commanding officer and must meet the minimum requirements, expressed or implied, that this position entails.

Chaplains can be powerful leaders, whose influence on others has been profound and inspiring under the most difficult of conditions. Commanders know that just the presence of chaplains can be a help to soldiers in battlefield conditions, because the chaplains represent a higher power, a hope, and comfort. The idea was that if the chaplain was on the battlefield, God was on the battlefield.

---

[26] Thompson, *European Antecedents*, 1:12-13.

# THE REVOLUTIONARY WAR

During the American Revolution, many clergy and chaplains distinguished themselves on the battlefield, and some clergy even led their own congregations into battle. There were fifteen chaplains in twenty-three regiments when Washington took command of the Continental Army.

The Reverend William Emerson, grandfather to Ralph Waldo Emerson, is credited with being the first chaplain of the Revolutionary War. As a pastor in Concord, Massachusetts, he was one of the first people to respond to the British attack of 1776. When the time for battle drew near, he walked up and down the lines, carrying his rifle, and encouraging and calming the soldiers.[27]

Chaplains lived and worked alongside the people they ministered to and shared in their dangers. John Rosbrugh was the first chaplain killed at the second battle of Trenton in 1777.

But of course, they did more than fight alongside their constituents. Chaplains held daily worship services, preached on Sundays, cared for the sick and wounded, conducted burials, and provided counsel and fellowship. One chaplain also served as the regimental surgeon during the American Revolution, and others worked in hospitals, or among the Indians. One chaplain was the German *chaplain at large* for all German troops, and there was a Headquarters Division chaplain.

In September 1756, Colonel George Washington repeatedly asked Governor Dinwiddie of Virginia for a regimental chaplain: "The want of a chaplain does, I humbly conceive, reflect dishonor upon the regiment, as all other officers are allowed. The gentlemen of the corps are sensible to this, and did propose to support one at their private

---

[27] Thompson, *European Antecedents*, 1:91.

expense. But I think it would have a more graceful appearance were he appointed as others are."[28]

After exchanging several letters, Washington wrote, "It is a hardship upon the Regiment, I think, to be denied a Chaplain. . . . We shou'd also be glad if our Chaplain was appointed, and that a Gentleman of sober, serious and religious deportment were chosen for this important Trust! Otherwise, we shou'd be better without."[29] Finally, seven months later, a chaplain was funded out of the Virginia Assembly's Supply Bill, but still no chaplain was appointed, and they ended up doing without. Apparently, Washington did have local clergy hold Sunday services, when they were available, but that did not meet the need of having a chaplain among the soldiers.

I've often wondered that George Washington kept insisting on an official chaplain to minister to him and the men in his regiment. He was a very devout Christian and believed in God. But George seemed to know he was in a providential position, especially since he came through some terrible battles unscathed, while other officers and friends fell at his side.

A little over a year before he wrote Governor Dinwiddie, he was on a campaign with General Braddock. On July 9th, 1755, General Braddock, with his aide the twenty-three year old Lieutenant Colonel George Washington, and one thousand, four hundred men crossed the Monongahela River as they advanced to attack the French and Indians at Fort Duquesne. The expedition accidentally ran into a large force of French and Indians, who opened fire on them. In the opening moments of the battle, many of the officers were

---

[28] Thompson, *European Antecedents*, 1:57.
[29] Thompson, *European Antecedents*, 1:58.

killed, and in the smoke and confusion of the surprise attack, most of the soldiers ran.[30]

Half the force was killed or wounded, and out of eighty-six officers, twenty-six were killed. Four days later General Braddock died of his wounds, and George Washington wrote a letter to his brother: "By the all-powerful dispensations of Providence, I have been protected beyond all human probability or expectation; for I had four bullets through my coat, and two horses shot under me, and escaped unhurt, although death was leveling my companions on every side of me."[31]

The Reverend James Wilmer, an Anglican clergyman from Maryland, became Chaplain of the United States Senate in 1809, while continuing to serve in his church. In 1813, he became a chaplain in the regular Army, and he was the only chaplain killed in April 1814, during the War of 1812 (The war with Britain started in 1812, which is where it got its name, and lasted a little over two years). It was Rev. Wilmer who proposed that the American version of the Anglican Church be renamed as the *Protestant Episcopal Church*.[32]

In 1838, the Army authorized post chaplains, which included the West Point Military Academy. Although the number of posts grew from fifteen to thirty by 1849, half of the posts did not have chaplains and many local commanders hired, at their own or post expense, local clergy and missionaries who were part of the westward expansion.[33]

---

[30] National Park Service, "The Braddock Campaign," 2006. *National Park Service Web*. http://www.nps.gov/fone/braddock.htm (27 Oct 2006).
[31] Thompson, *European Antecedents*, 1:56.
[32] Herman A. Norton, *Struggling for Recognition: The United States Army Chaplaincy 1791-1865* (6 vols.; Honolulu, HI: University Press of the Pacific), 2:16-17.
[33] Norton, *Struggling for Recognition*, 2:45.

When a chaplain was appointed to a frontier Army post, his duties usually included being the school master for the children of soldiers, the soldiers themselves, and local settlers. These chaplains also held services in the community, officiated at different events, visited sick prisoners and soldiers, managed the post gardens and the library, and provided legal counsel.

At the military academy at West Point, the chaplain was expected to perform the usual ministerial duties of preaching and holding services, but was also supposed to teach geography, ethics, and history.[34] Some were up to the dual task, and some were not.

## THE CIVIL WAR – ADVENT OF MODERN CHAPLAINCY

If the Civil War is known as the first modern war, then it is arguably the birth of modern chaplaincy.[35] It is estimated that three thousand chaplains were appointed by the Union and six hundred to one thousand served on the Confederate side. On both sides, chaplains served in regiments, posts, prisons, and hospitals. In addition, there were many local clergy and layman who held services for the soldiers but had no official affiliation with the Army.

In this war, chaplains were not encouraged to fight, although many did, and spiritual and religious ministry was emphasized. They held their usual services and rituals, and visited the sick and wounded, taught classes, wrote and mailed letters for the soldiers, acted as bankers, ambulance drivers, legal counselors, and recruiters. It was not unusual to find Catholic and Protestant chaplains performing services together and sharing duties.

---

[34] Norton, *Struggling for Recognition*, 2:24.
[35] William E. Dickens, Jr., *Answering the Call: The Story of the U.S. Military Chaplaincy from the Revolution through the Civil War* (Dissertation.com, 1998), 142-3.

On both sides of the war, there were over one million casualties, six hundred thousand deaths, and three hundred thousand who died of disease. So chaplains found the aid stations, surgery tents, and hospitals to be one of their primary places of duty. Many were actually assigned to the surgeon or assistant surgeon during battles.

Every night up to ten soldiers died, and early in the morning the chaplain would start his day by performing funerals for those to be buried on the grounds. Chaplain Jerome Spilman, of the Fifth Iowa Calvary, wrote his wife in January of 1862 and gave a short account of his feelings and challenges in the field with his regiment:

> I would [sic] souldiering very well if I did not see so much suffering and death, but Oh what sights I witness daily in the hospitals and among the sick. Was it not that my trust of my trust in God, I would turn away from all such scenes forever. But my mission is to the suffering, and only let me smooth their pillow in the hour of death, and I am amply rewarded for all my labor.[36]

During the Civil War, there were a large number of Roman Catholic chaplains, the first Jewish chaplains, African-American chaplains, and Indian chaplains. After much debate and lobbying, Rabbi Frankel was commissioned by Abraham Lincoln in 1862 to serve with the 5th Philadelphia Regiment. The Reverend Henry McNeal Turner was the first African-American chaplain and served the 1st Regiment, U.S. Colored Troops. During the war, twelve colored regiments would have their own chaplains. Unaguskie was the chaplain for the Cherokee Battalion of North Carolina, and Mrs. Ella E. Gibson Hobart was a chaplain, temporarily, for the 1st Wisconsin Regiment.[37] Although President Lincoln did not object to Mrs. Hobart being the regimental chaplain, he left the decision of her employment up to Secretary of War Stanton, who had her removed after a few months.

---

[36] Dickens, *Answering the Call*, 126.
[37] Dickens, *Answering the Call*, 145.

There are many instances of black soldiers serving in the Confederate army, and there was a Tennessee regiment of white soldiers that had a black chaplain. Uncle Lewis preached regularly and ministered to the sick and injured, and he was highly respected. Apparently, he served in this position throughout the war. The following article is from the Richmond, Virginia, *Religious Herald*, September 10, 1863:

> To the Confederate army goes the distinction of having the first black to minister to white troops: "A correspondent of the SOLDIER'S FRIEND mentions a Tennessee regiment which has no chaplain; but an old negro, "Uncle Lewis," preaches two or three times a week at night. He is heard with respectful attention -- and for earnestness, zeal and sincerity, can be surpassed by none. Two or three revivals have followed his preaching in the regiment. What will the wise Christian patriots out of the army, who denounce those who wish to see competent negroes allowed to preach, as tainted with anti-slaveryism, say with regard to the true Southern feeling of that regiment, which has fought unflinchingly from Shiloh to Murfreesboro?"[38]

## EARLY HOSPITAL CHAPLAINCY

Hospital chaplaincy, as a recognized ministry, began during the Civil War. President Lincoln encouraged Congress to pass a law allowing a regular Army chaplain at each permanent hospital. It took almost a year for Congress to pass the bill, and it placed hospital chaplains under the Surgeon General. In response to this new duty, the Surgeon General had his brother, Chaplain J. Pinkney Hammond, write a guide for all hospital chaplains called, the *Army Chaplain's Manual*, which included hymns and services. During the war, over five hundred chaplains served in the hospitals. Although there were one hundred, ninety-two hospitals, only one hundred, seventy-three were ever staffed at one time.[39]

---

[38] Genealogy Forum, "U.S. Civil War History & Genealogy Compiled References Regarding Black Confederates," *Genealogy Forum Web.*
http://www.genealogyforum.com/gfaol/resource/Military/BlackConfederates.htm (10 Dec 2006).
[39] Norton, *Struggling for Recognition*, 2:114-6.

The medical profession was in the midst of its *Age of Reason* and enlightened scientific methodology in the treatment of patients. Many physicians did not see the need for religious ministrations in the hospitals, and some were openly hostile to the very idea. In the military, some hospital commanders were often indifferent. They did not understand the idea of holistic healing, and thought the work of ministers was a basic waste of time. But if the chaplain moved slowly yet confidently in his work with the patients and staff, in time he could win over the skeptical.[40]

At the beginning of the Civil War, the Sisters of Charity and the Sisters of Mercy of New York sent seventy-five nuns to work in Army hospitals performing the physical and spiritual work needed to comfort and help the patients. The sisters helped with the obvious physical needs, but also prayed with soldiers, gave them religious literature, and prepared them for baptism. By the end of the war, six hundred sisters from eleven orders served the wounded and dying (Sisters of Providence, Sisters of St Joseph, Daughters of Charity of St Vincent de Paul, Sisters of Charity, Sisters of Mercy, Sisters of Our Lady of Mercy, Sisters of St Ursula,; Sisters of the Poor of St Francis, Sisters of Our Lady of Mt Carmel, Sisters of St Dominic, Sisters of the Holy Cross).[41] Today, the Providence and Franciscan healthcare systems are a testament to their continued devotion to the healing ministry.

---

[40] Norton, *Struggling for Recognition*, 2:122.
[41] Norton, *Struggling for Recognition*, 2:123.

# AFTER THE CIVIL WAR

After the Civil War and the disbandment of the armies, there was only a small contingent

of chaplains in the posts from West Point to the Southwest. They had the usual range of

pastoral duties including teaching children and soldiers, managing the garden,

commissary, bakery, and acting as librarian, treasurer, attorney, and organizing

temperance societies to curb drinking among soldiers.

Although some chaplains were adversely affected by Indian atrocities on settlers,

most saw them as a significant part of their ministry. Like missionaries to foreign

countries, many chaplains saw it as their duty to take Christianity to the *natives*.

> While obstacles were many and almost insurmountable, efforts were constantly
> made, most times successfully, to establish congregations in the Indian
> communities. In a few instances the Indians themselves took the initiative and
> invited chaplains to conduct worship in their midst. The fruits of those endeavors
> more than repaid the effort expended and attempts of the two groups to live
> together in peaceful relationship became more dependable. For their part the
> Indians were constantly giving chaplains timely notices of proposed raids which
> prevented garrisons from being surprised; because of this general massacres were
> averted.[42]

Although most Catholic chaplains held worship services and taught English and

catechism classes among the Indians, Catholic Chaplain Edward J. Vattmann went a step

further and created the Sioux Soldier's Vocabulary, and translated other textbooks into

the Sioux language.[43] The book was a valuable tool for managing Sioux Indian affairs.

Chaplain Leander Kerr of Fort Leavenworth spent time learning the languages,

rituals, and customs of the local Indians of the Kansas Missouri territory. Whenever the

---

[42] Norton, *Struggling for Recognition*, 2:54.
[43] Stover, *Up from Handymen*, 3:40.

garrison rode out to confront the Indians during a disturbance, Chaplain Kerr would ride along, and thus was often able to calm things down and avoid fighting.[44]

Chaplain Andrew D. Mitchell was the first chaplain of the United States Military Prison at Fort Leavenworth. His ministry to the inmates included religious services, creating and managing a library, counseling, teaching, and raising up tutors from the prisoners to teach other inmates.

## WORLD WAR I

When World War I started, there were one hundred, forty-six chaplains in the Army (seventy-four Regular Army, seventy-two National Guard), and during the war the ranks swelled to two thousand, three hundred, and sixty-three. But the Army headquarters quickly lost track of where they were all assigned in the American Expeditionary Force. So General Pershing had his own pastor, the Rt. Reverend Charles Henry Bent, an Episcopal Bishop, commissioned a Major and assigned the task of organizing the chaplains in Europe: figuring out where they were, who they were, and their denominations. Chaplain Bent created the chaplaincy corps based on the British and Canadian models. He had the experienced chaplains promoted and assigned to higher levels, while giving them the task of managing the less experienced chaplains, and the religious needs and morale of the soldiers under them.[45]

Chaplains often rode with the medical aid stations to provide care to the frontline combat soldiers, wounded and dying, and the medical staff. After battles, they assisted in the recovery of the dead and performed burials. Twenty-three chaplains died, eleven in

---

[44] Norton, *Struggling for Recognition*, 2:57.
[45] Robert L. Gushwa, *The Best and Worst of Times: The United States Army Chaplaincy 1920-1945* (6 vols.; Washington DC: Office of the Chief of Chaplains, Department of the Army), 4:5-6.

battle, and they earned many awards for bravery and distinguished service. At the memorial service where the Distinguished Service Cross (DSC) was awarded posthumously to Chaplain Coleman E. O'Flaherty, his commander said that the medal actually stood for, *Died in the Service of Christ.*[46]

As is the custom in the Army following a war, most of the soldiers were discharged, and by 1920 the chaplain ranks had shrunk to one hundred and twenty-five. But the chaplain branch and the organization that Chaplain Bent created remained, and the Chaplain School was started.

## AFTER WORLD WAR I

During the Great Depression, the Civilian Conservation Corps (CCC) was managed by the Army and over three hundred chaplains, active duty and reserves, worked in the many camps ministering to the people who worked on the numerous projects across the country. The CCC performed emergency work (fighting forest fires, flood control), helped in cleaning up after storms, and carved many of the hiking trails still used today in the Rocky Mountains, Appalachians, and Sierra Nevada mountains.

Just like chaplains in the Army, the CCC chaplains went wherever the camps were set up and ministered to the needs of the workers. Chaplain Alva J. Brasted wrote:

> It has been my good fortune to be closely associated with the religious work of the Civilian Conservation Corps. . . . To go about the country visiting the C.C.C. personnel, giving character building lectures, holding conferences . . . I speak not only for myself but for all our chaplains when I say that the most remarkable experience any man can have is to help these boys in their personal problems, and to direct them in the way of right thinking and right habits, in a word to help them develop in character and to become more like the men they want to be and ought to be.[47]

---

[46] Stover, *Up from Handymen*, 3:194.
[47] Gushwa, *The Best and Worst of Times*, 4:60-1.

## WORLD WAR II – A SPIRITUAL BATTLE

In 1939, America's army was considered smaller and less efficient than Poland's. After Germany defeated Poland in September of 1939, President Franklin D. Roosevelt wisely, and with great foresight, decided to start increasing the military's people and equipment. From September 1939 until the Japanese surrender in September 1945, nine thousand, one hundred, and seventeen chaplains were on active duty. With Army ranks at over eight million during the war, the ratio of chaplains to soldiers was almost 1:1,000.[48]

Although there was a pacifist movement before the war and much debate about whether it was moral or immoral, the Japanese attack on Pearl Harbor ended all of that. Chaplain Terence P. Finnegan was preparing for Sunday Mass when he saw the Japanese planes diving on Pearl Harbor. Chaplain Alvin Katt was at Wheeler Field for his Protestant Sunday service, when the Japanese planes started staffing the flightline and his new chapel. Chaplain Elmer Tiedt was at Hickam Field when it got strafed, and his assistant was killed in front of the church altar set up on the flightline in an old wooden hangar. Chaplain Harry P. Richmond, a Jewish chaplain, was listening to the radio when the attack started. They all headed for the hospital and ministered to the injured and dying.[49]

The Army Chief of Chaplains during this period was Catholic Chaplain (Major General) William R. Arnold. He believed the war was a spiritual battle and said, "We are at war with pagans, atheists, and Satan himself."[50] Although chaplains were considered

---

[48] Gushwa, *The Best and Worst of Times*, 4:99.
[49] Gushwa, *The Best and Worst of Times*, 4:102-4.
[50] Gushwa, *The Best and Worst of Times*, 4:105.

noncombatants, he allowed that there were times when it might be necessary to take up arms: "If there is a need to defend his cause or himself in battle, let him take it as his duty. A dead chaplain is no good to his men."[51]

The work and role of chaplains was never greater than in World War II, because the military leaders also saw the war, primarily, as a spiritual battle. General Eisenhower wrote, "The Allied soldier sees himself as a defender of those great precepts of humanitarianism preached by Christ and exemplified in the way of life for which all true democracies stand. He sees this conflict as a war between greed and selfishness and love of power today typified in Nazism, Fascism and Shintoism."[52]

Of all the many duties chaplains had, the primary, and perhaps most important, was that of counselor. As men were impersonally shuffled about the theaters of war, a person could sit down with a chaplain and confide in them despite rank or problem. Whatever the location or setting, the chaplain recognized them as individuals and offered guidance, comfort, and hope. Because chaplains honored these conversations as sacred and confidential, and could not be called to testify at a court-martial concerning what they heard, many men brought all of their problems to the chaplain, even the military ones.

---

[51] Gushwa, *The Best and Worst of Times*, 4:105.
[52] Gushwa, *The Best and Worst of Times*, 4:130-1.

"Greater love has no one than this, that he lay down his life for his friends."[53]

In the line of fire, many Catholic chaplains died on the battlefield giving grievously wounded soldiers the last rites. In an attempt to be where they were needed most, four hundred and seventy-eight chaplains died.

The troop transport ship, Dorchester, was hit by a German submarine torpedo at one in the morning on February 3, 1943. As the ship quickly went down, four chaplains, (Lt. George L. Fox, Methodist; Lt. Alexander D. Goode, Jewish; Lt. John P. Washington, Catholic; and Lt. Clark V. Poling, Reformed), gave their life jackets to others and helped soldiers get into the life boats. They stood on the deck with their arms linked together, praying, as the ship slipped below the water.[54]

Before the Dorchester went down, Chaplain Poling had written his father, "I know I shall have your prayers, but please don't pray simply that God will keep me safe. War is dangerous business. Pray that God will make me adequate!"[55]

Chaplains were captured in both theaters of war, Pacific and Europe, and put into prisoner of war camps. Under the Japanese they were thought to be spreading propaganda, and there are many stories of incredible brutality. In time, some of the Japanese prisons became more lenient and allowed more freedoms for religious observances. Under the Germans some of the chaplains enjoyed all the freedoms they needed to minister to their fellow prisoners.

---

[53] John 15:13.
[54] Gushwa, *The Best and Worst of Times*, 4:127-9.
[55] Gushwa, *The Best and Worst of Times*, 4:127.

## DENOMINATIONS REPRESENTED DURING WORLD WAR II

During the war, the following denominations were represented: Advent Christian; Baptist Churches; Baptist-General Association of Regular North; Baptist General Conference of North America; German Baptist; Seventh-Day Baptist; Swedish Baptist; Brethren, General Conference; Brethren, Old Constitution; Brethren, Progressive; Christian and Missionary Alliance; Christian Scientist; Church of God, Indiana; Church of God, Pennsylvania; Eastern Orthodox; Episcopal, Reformed; Evangelical Missionary Covenant; Evangelical, Congregational; Evangelical, Free; Foursquare; Friends; Greek Orthodox; Independent Fundamental Churches of America; Methodist, Free; Methodist, South; Methodist, Wesleyan; Moravian; Norwegian and Danish Evangelical Free Church; Mormon; Pentecostal Holiness; Presbyterian, Associated Reformed; Presbyterian, Bible; Presbyterian, Church of Canada; Presbyterian, Cumberland; Presbyterian, Orthodox; Roman Catholic; United Grace and T.E.A.; Univeralists.[56]

Because the predominant faith in the military in the past had been Christian, the inclusivity emphasis was more in the area of denominations rather than faith groups. But in recent times, and in an ever expanding effort to meet the diverse spiritual and religious needs of the people in the military, the Chaplain Corps now accepts over one hundred religious denominations and faith groups. It was only as recent as July of 2004, that a Buddhist chaplain was commissioned for full-time service.

---

[56] Gushwa, *The Best and Worst of Times*, 4:100-1, 210.

## AFTER WORLD WAR II

After the war, Jewish chaplains worked with the people coming out of the concentration camps, helping them find families, start synagogues, and place orphans in homes and orphanages. American chaplains worked with German prisoner of war chaplains to help provide relief to civilians in the war-torn regions.

In 1947, the Department of Veteran Affairs added chaplains to their hospital staff, and the Air Force and Navy started their own chaplaincy schools. The number of chaplains did not drop as precipitously as in past wars, because the world moved into the Cold War period and the threat of Communism loomed. But the number of chaplains was down to seven hundred, seventy-five as the Korean War started in 1950.


## THE KOREAN WAR – COMMUNISM VERSUS CHRISTIANITY

Missionaries brought Christianity to the Korean peninsula in the 1700's. As the Communists advanced southward, they persecuted Korean Christians and burned down their churches.

As North Korean troops began to overrun American positions in the middle of July 1950, Chaplain Herman G. Felhoelter, Roman Catholic, helped carry wounded soldiers to the rear positions. One hundred men were trying to carry thirty wounded, and as they topped a hill, it became apparent that they would soon be overpowered. Chaplain Felhoelter convinced the medical officer to get the men away while he stayed with the wounded, and the able-bodied soldiers ran for their lives. One of the fleeing soldiers, a sergeant, looked back with his binoculars as the North Koreans came upon the pitiful group. He reported that the enemy soldiers shot the wounded and Chaplain Felhoelter as he prayed with them.[57]

Chaplain Arthur E. Mills, Advent Christian, with the 1st Cavalry Division's 8th Regiment, overheard a remark in the command center that wounded soldiers would have to be abandoned as a unit withdrew. Chaplain Mills had served in World War II, and as he ran out and jumped into a jeep, he yelled, "This is the way we did it in the last war!" and roared off. With his jeep, he rescued a load of men and was himself wounded.[58]

Some chaplain prisoners of war died in captivity, because they were abused for being Christians, and thirteen chaplains died in the conflict.

On the television series *Mash 4077*, about a Mobile Army Surgical Hospital in the Korean War, Father Mulcahy, the Catholic chaplain, often typified what a chaplain really does and who he really is, despite the Hollywood tendency toward stereotyping. He struggled with issues of faith, the lack of promotion, performed services, taught classes, helped the unit get much needed supplies, served in the surgical theater, counseled soldiers, ministered to the sick and dying and the staff, helped a local orphanage, and inspirationally modeled the Christian life at all times.


THE VIETNAM WAR

A soldier in Vietnam responded to a chaplain survey and wrote these words that capture the sentiments of soldiers all through history:

> The chaplain was essential to the morale of the combat soldier. He often spent
> time with my troops and on several occasions was with us in combat. The

---

[57] Rodger R. Venzke, *Confidence in Battle, Inspiration in Peace: The United States Army Chaplaincy 1945-1975*, 6 vols. (Washington, DC: Office of the Chief of Chaplains, Department of the Army, 1977), 68-9.
[58] Venzke, *Confidence in Battle*, 70.

chaplains were there to give comfort to wounded soldiers and to those who had just lost a good friend. For the soldier to see a chaplain living under the same conditions that he was experiencing enhanced the credibility of the chaplain when performing counseling or giving spiritual comfort.[59]

Army Regulation 165-20 was published during the Vietnam war and describes the duties of chaplains. It is very enlightening and shows the scope of their responsibilities, duties, and leadership:

> The primary mission of the chaplain is to provide for the religious and moral needs of military personnel, their families, and authorized civilians with special attention given to the welfare of the soldier. In accomplishing his mission, the chaplain will seek to develop a relationship of trust and mutual respect between himself and all members of the command. So far as practicable, each chaplain will provide a dynamic and comprehensive program of chaplain activities to include generally the following areas:
>
> a. Religious services. These services will include . . . services of worship, religious missions, religious retreats, marriages, baptisms, funerals, and other sacraments, rites, and/or ordinances.
>
> b. Religious education.
>
> c. Pastoral care . . . The chaplain will seek to:
>
> (1) Develop a pastoral relationship with members of the command, by participating in activities of the command, by visiting soldiers during duty and off-duty hours without interfering with the soldier's official duties or his privacy.
>
> (2) Make himself available to all members of the command for interviews, guidance, counseling, and spiritual help.
>
> (3) Assist in the rehabilitation of personnel in confinement by counseling and instruction and by cooperating with members of the staff.
>
> (4) Provide spiritual support and help to the sick and their families by visitations, counseling, appropriate religious ministrations, and other appropriate assistance as a member of the healing team.[60]

---

[59] Henry F. Ackermann, *He Was Always There: The U.S. Army Chaplain Ministry in the Vietnam Conflict* (Washington DC: Office of the Chief of Chaplains, Department of the Army, 1989), 19.
[60] Ackermann, *He Was Always There*, v.

As in previous conflicts, chaplains went wherever the troops went. So in 1962, chaplains were among the first soldiers to enter Vietnam. Like Methodist clergy circuit riders of the 1800's, they traveled from outpost to outpost, camp to camp, fire base to fire base, by any means possible, conducting services and ministering to soldiers. Chaplains often organized humanitarian aid for the Vietnamese who were suffering. Over an eleven year period, thirteen chaplains died.

At the height of the war, there were three hundred chaplains in Vietnam. The ratio of troops to chaplains was generally seven hundred to one, but combat, combat support units, and hospitals got priority. In addition, there was a serious lack of African-American chaplains given the number of African-American soldiers fighting in the country. The Director of Personnel in the Office of the Chief of Chaplains Headquarters wrote:

"When black troops don't see a black chaplain they conclude we don't have any and don't want any. We have 56 on duty now and not a chance of getting any more at this time. We're also running into a problem on Vietnam assignments as practically all of these 56 have had two short tours in recent years."[61] The Army's plan was to have soldiers do no more than two short tours to Vietnam, unless they volunteered for additional tours.

At this time, the Department of the Army decided that only officers should make next-of-kin notifications in the event a soldier was killed or missing in action. This duty usually fell to a junior officer in the area of notification and the local chaplain. Many chaplains stated that among their many duties, the toughest duty was next-of-kin notifications: Where chaplains were welcomed and encouraged in other areas, their presence at the front door of a home spelled disaster for the family.

---

[61] Ackermann, *He Was Always There*, 43.

Being a good leader means influencing people, and I believe a corollary to that would be that a good leader is a good team member. In 1967, Chaplain James D. Bruton was the chaplain for MASH 3 and was an integral, vital part of the healing team. He wrote:

> When wounded came in, I felt it my duty to be there to assist the patient through his pain and fears. I spoke directly into the patient's ear, quietly and unemotionally, reassuring him that he was safe and receiving excellent care. I would often say a prayer for God's protection and healing . . . I would explain everything the doctor was doing . . . and this was reassuring . . . knowing what was going on . . . seemed to calm the patient and allow the medical team to perform their work without undue emotional involvement on the part of the patient.[62]

Because of anti-war sentiments that raged across the country, chaplains were sought out by soldiers wanting to claim conscientious objector status based on religious convictions, so they could leave the war and go home. The Army gave chaplains the responsibility of interviewing the soldiers to determine the sincerity of their religious beliefs. In addition, the widespread use of drugs during the 1960's and the racial unrest, meant that chaplains were on the leading edge of these issues by providing drug and race relations education and counseling.

Chaplains of the Vietnam conflict stated that their strength came from "their faith and faithfulness to ministry, their presence in the face of death, a willingness to learn from those to whom they ministered, and a realization that they did not know all the answers."[63] In the leadership paradigm, this statement captures it all: Faith as a foundation, faithfulness to their calling, being fully present to those in need, a humility based on a willingness to learn, and knowing they did not have all the answers. Wherever chaplains successfully serve, this will always be true.

---

[62] Ackermann, *He Was Always There*, 85.
[63] Ackermann, *He Was Always There*, 92.

"The chaplain's ministry remembers the past, deals in present reality, prepares for the future, and always touches reality."[64] It's that *touching reality* that gives chaplain leadership such power and influence.

## AFTER VIETNAM

After the Vietnam war, there were many changes in the country, the military, and the chaplaincy. In 1974, the first woman chaplain was commissioned in the Army, and there were married couples, where both were in the chaplaincy. Chaplains now found themselves dealing more with HIV prevention and education, race relations and education, suicide prevention, marriage enrichment classes, drug abuse education, family abuse, and grief counseling.

## THE BALKANS

Balkan is the Turkish word for *mountain* or *highland slope.* The Balkans consists of the countries of Slovenia, Croatia, Bosnia-Hercegovina, Volvodina, Serbia, Montenegro, Albania, Macedonia, Bulgaria, Romania, and Greece. Sometimes Hungary and Eastern Turkey are included.

The Greeks and Romans found the people of this mountainous region to be contentious and volatile. Over time, the Roman Catholic and Eastern Orthodox churches had a great influence on these people, but in 1389, the combined armies of Serbia, Albania, Montenegro, and Bosnia were defeated by the Ottomans. In 1453, Constantinople fell to the Ottoman Muslims. Bosnia and Herzegovina were controlled by

---

[64] Ackermann, *He Was Always There*, 1.

the Muslims from 1463 until 1878, and Albania was controlled by them from 1482 until as recently as 1912.

From 1995 to 2005, the United States participated in a United Nations peacemaking/peacekeeping mission in the Balkans. Although there was always tension between the Roman Catholic, Eastern Orthodox, and Serbian Orthodox people, the fighting in this region was based on the historic angers associated with the invasion of the Muslims and the atrocities that followed. The people of this part of the world seem to hold old grievances close to their heart, where they are able to fester and grow. Subsequently, after President Tito died in 1980, Yugoslavia broke up into separate countries again, and in 1990, Serbia and Croatia started fighting. Serbia broke away in June 1991, and Milosevic became president of Serbia declaring the desire to form an ethnic state of Greater Serbia. When Bosnia and other countries rebelled at this idea, he decided to eliminate all non-Serbians. Centuries of Muslim hatred surfaced, and whole villages of people were destroyed.

"Today, it is a war fanned by vivid religious memories of the past and a desire to get revenge at any cost. This is evident in the population cleansing that is currently taking place. It is not just ethnic cleansing; it is religious and the intent is to inflict as much pain and suffering as possible."[65]

As part of the United Nations, U.S. troops entered Bosnia in 1996 (including my son). Chaplains found themselves working alongside multinational chaplains in a multi-religious region. By 1998, there were fifty chaplains representing thirty-eight nations.[66]

---

[65] Kenneth E. Lawson, *Faith and Hope in the War-Torn Land: The US Army Chaplaincy in the Balkans 1995-2005* (Ft Leavenworth, KS: Combat Studies Institute Press, 2006), 7.
[66] Lawson, *Faith and Hope*, 69.

When they started constructing chapels, they could not put up crosses because the crosses

offended the Jewish and Muslim United Nations soldiers and many civilians.

Chaplain (CPT) Ronald Cooper had a special ministry to the senior leaders in his

camp. "We developed a 'Top Gun Leaders' ministry to commanders and staff officers.

We studied together a leadership book each month. Then we met for dinner and discussed

the book. Then I would teach a 1-hour class on leadership. We did this for the 6 months

we were in Bosnia."[67]

Chaplains played a major leadership role in defusing ethnic tensions. Lutheran

Chaplain (MAJ) Michael Lembke met regularly with Christian clergy of the Croatia and

Serbia, and Muslim clergy of Bosnia. They were amazed that the different United

Nations religious groups shared the same military chapel.[68]

There was a leadership gap in the United Nations peacekeeping mission that was

filled by chaplains. The chaplains saw a leadership need and stepped forward to fill it:

> US Army chaplains serving throughout the Balkans from 1995 to 2005 were
> essential in the reconciliation process for the diverse religious populations.
> Clearly, the role of the chaplain as a religious adviser to the commanders, long an
> expectation in the military, was solidified and enhanced. . . . Army chaplains
> networked with local clergy and political leaders, brought rival religious factions
> to clergy events, promoted harmony among rival groups, and encouraged
> forgiveness and acceptance by long-standing belligerents.[69]

Within the formal, military, peacekeeping system they found themselves,

chaplains were advising, teaching, coaching, counseling, networking, encouraging and

mentoring others. In the clergy environment, they were the leaders, while at the same

time, they could be advising as a subordinate leader to the unit commander. It was

---

[67] Lawson, *Faith and Hope*, 82.
[68] ibid.
[69] Lawson, *Faith and Hope*, 171.

dynamic and flowing and powerful. Because of their leadership and actions, chaplains were highly instrumental in the successful completion of this peacekeeping mission.

Chaplain Lembke said, "Who better than a chaplain to talk about healing and reconciliation in a peacekeeping environment."[70]

My son, Joshua, was in the Balkans at this time with 1-1 Cavalry. Their Protestant chaplain wanted to get in good with the guys, so he allowed them to take pictures of himself with a blowup doll on his lap. It made people laugh, and some of the soldiers thought he was pretty cool. But most of the soldiers in the unit lost respect for him as a minister, and my son reports that his ministry after that became ineffective.

AIRBORNE SCHOOL

During World War II, Episcopal Chaplain Raymond S. Hall was the first chaplain to complete the five weeks of airborne training and jump with his paratroopers. When a reporter asked Chaplain Hall why he jumped, he said, "It increases attendance at church, and the men can talk to me now."[71] Jumping out of perfectly good airplanes created a special camaraderie among the jumpers, and airborne chaplains quickly earned their respect.

When I was in airborne school at Fort Benning, Georgia, in February 1987, a chaplain was in training right alongside all of the soldiers. After five weeks of intense training, we boarded a C-130 cargo ship and climbed to 1,500 feet. As the Jump Master opened the door and the roar of the passing wind filled the cargo hold, I began to experience a low-grade panic. There would be one last opportunity to avoid jumping out

---

[70] Lawson, *Faith and Hope*, 172.
[71] Gushwa, *The Best and Worst of Times*, 4:112.

of this perfectly flying airplane by stepping aside at the door. But as we stood up and shuffled forward, a few women went out the door first, followed by a few young guys of about eighteen, and then the chaplain. When it was my turn I knew I had to jump because of the example given by the women, children, and the clergy. I reasoned that even if all their chutes didn't open, I would still have to go out the door just to keep my pride—and I did, five times.

## DESERT STORM

Over five hundred and sixty chaplains served in Desert Storm. They held regular services on Sundays, and went around visiting troop locations to provide comfort and counsel. I served in this war as an Armor officer (tanks). After we liberated Kuwait City from the Iraqis in February 2001, we settled in to help the Kuwaitis rebuild their infrastructure, starting with electricity and water for the hospital. The chaplain went around from unit to unit briefing the soldiers on the effects of war. The following is my March 23, 1991 letter that I wrote home from the north side of Kuwait City, where we were camped after the fighting:

> The Chaplain talked about returning to the families – about how you would've changed, and I would've changed. I know you will be and are much more self-confident, I can hear it in your voice. I'm prepared for that – ha! But he talked about the combat and post-combat stress we're going through. I suspect, and you should be prepared for, a husband who will be somewhat depressed upon return – Not because of the return, but a symptom of my present condition. Like, its part of the "healing" process – something I will be aware of. I'll not try to be a pain, but I can see it coming. I'm flying along here at 10,000 feet, going mach 1 with a dry battery. Someday I've gotta land, except I'll plow into the runway – and depending on how hard and fast I hit, will depend on how severe my reaction will be.

So you foam the runway. I'll try not to clip any tree tops on final approach. At times, even now, I get immersed in a "sadness," close to tears. But I prop myself up, straighten my back, square my shoulders, and march on.

# CHAPTER 3 – OVERVIEW OF VARIOUS CHAPLAINCIES

The most obvious and well known chaplaincy positions are in healthcare, the military,

and with police and fire departments, but there are many others. In this section, I want to

briefly describe most of the chaplaincies, understanding that people of many faiths and

denominations serve as chaplains in these positions and other places.

## BUDDHIST CHAPLAINS

Buddhism has been described by Buddhists as a religion, a philosophy, and as both.

There are many different Buddhist traditions and sects, and variations within sects:

Mahayana, Hinayana, Pureland, Theravada, Tibetan, Zen, and many others. Among them

are overlaps in philosophy and practice: Zen uses Mahayana teaching, Theravada uses

Hinayana teaching, Tibetan uses Mahayana and Hinayana teaching.[72]

> Therefore we ask, if Buddhism is not a religion, what then is it? Our reply is:
> Buddhism is a way of life, a philosophy, a psychology, a way of thinking, through
> which we may ourselves take on the responsibility of determining how our life-
> bearing kamma (karma) will work out for us. Meditation is one of the procedures
> of mental discipline and purification through which we may begin to learn such
> responsibility.[73]

As a hospital chaplain, it is not necessary to know all of the different beliefs,

although learning about them will make you a better chaplain.[74] But for ministry to the

---

[72] Buddhist Information of North America, "What is Tibetan Buddhism?" *Buddhist Information Web.*
http://www.buddhistinformation.com/tibetan/what_is_tibetan_buddhism.htm (17 Nov 2006).
[73] Dorothy Figen, "Is Buddhism a Religion?" *Buddhist Information Web.*
http://www.buddhistinformation.com/is_buddhism_a_religion1.htm (17 Nov 2006).
[74] Christopher Johnson and Marsha G. McGee, *How Different Religions View Death and Afterlife*, 2d ed.,
(Philadelphia: The Charles Press, 1998), passim.

Buddhist patient, the primary importance is to be fully present, non-judgmental, listening and hearing what they have to say and to their story, and offering comfort. Some Buddhist patients might want prayer, to be read to, simple conversation, or quiet presence. If the patient has not received visitors, ask them if they would like you to contact anyone: It might be family, a friend, or a Buddhist teacher of their beliefs. As with all chaplaincy ministry, in all these things let the patient guide you.

As a Buddhist chaplain, training in meditation, reflection, exploration, and self-discovery are well-suited to hospital and hospice ministry. When people are in crisis, the chaplain knows how to listen and look deeper in the moment as people face fears, decisions, and possibly contemplate their death.[75]

Many colleges and universities now have Buddhist chaplains. MIT Student News interviewed the campus Buddhist chaplain, Tenzin Priyadarshi: "He believed his religion's teachings and practices-including meditation-could help students cope with the pressures of attending one of the world's most prestigious universities. It is visibly the most stressed-out campus in the world," he said. "I believed I could help ease the suffering in students."[76] The Sati Center for Buddhist Studies has a Buddhist Chaplain Training Program taught at the Insight Mediation Center in Redwood City, California. It is open to people of all faiths (see links-Appendix A).

CIVIL AIR PATROL CHAPLAINS

The Civil Air Patrol was started December 1, 1941 by Gill Robb Wilson and Fiorello La Guardia, Mayor of New York City just a week before Pearl Harbor was bombed. During

---

[75] Annie Clay, Buddhist Hospice and Hospital Chaplain, Interview 13 Nov 2006.
[76] MIT Student News, "Dharma in the Dorm: MIT Hires Buddhist Chaplain," 22 June 2005. *MIT Student Web.* http://www.stnews.org/rlr-823.htm (27 Sep 2006).

World War II, the CAP airplanes flown by civilian volunteers, with their distinctive red

and yellow design, patrolled the coastlines of the United States. They spotted 173

German submarines, attacked fifty-seven, hit ten, and sank two. "A German commander

later confirmed that coastal U-boat operations were withdrawn from the United States

'because of those damned little red and yellow airplanes.' "[77]

The Civil Air Patrol (CAP) is the civilian auxiliary of the U.S. Air Force, and

their Chaplain Service is the largest all volunteer chaplaincy organization in the world.[78]

Most people are unfamiliar with the Civil Air Patrol and their modern mission. This

excerpt describes the modern day purposes and missions of the CAP:

> The five purposes of CAP, as stated in Article VI of its constitution, are:
>
> a. To provide an organization to encourage and aid American citizens in the contribution of their efforts, services, and resources in the development of aerospace and in the maintenance of aerospace supremacy.
> b. To encourage and develop, by example, the voluntary contribution of private citizens to the public welfare.
> c. To provide aviation and aerospace education and training, especially for its senior and cadet members.
> d. To encourage and foster civil aviation in local communities.
> e. To provide an organization of private citizens with adequate facilities to assist in meeting local and national emergencies.[79] The last purpose, which covers search and rescue, is how they are best known.
>
> The Mission of Civil Air Patrol
>
> In 1946, Congress granted a charter to Civil Air Patrol, charging its members with three missions. First, CAP was to promote aviation. As years passed, that mission expanded to include aerospace education as well. Second, CAP was to provide a training program to support the nation's youth in contributing to society and preparing for successful adult lives. Finally, CAP was to continue its emergency services, the work for which CAP is still best known today.[80]

---

[77] Civil Air Patrol, "Our History," *Civil Air Patrol Web*. http://www.cap.org (10 Dec 2006).

[78] Civil Air Patrol, "Info For Clergy," (10 Dec 2006).

[79] Civil Air Patrol Chaplains' Service, "Senior Member Training Program Specialty Track Study Guide," Civil Air Patrol Publication 221 (E), 10 Jan 1995. *Civil Air Patrol Web*. http://level2.cap.gov/documents/u_082503085137.pdf (10 Dec 2006), 6.

[80] Civil Air Patrol, "Our Programs, The Primary Missions of Civil Air Patrol," (10 Dec 2006).

The chaplaincy requirements for CAP are similar to other professional chaplaincy

organizations, but they are organized around the Air Force model.

> To become a CAP chaplain, you must be a fully qualified member of the clergy of your religious group with the appropriate educational background. Our chaplains come from all religious faith groups and include priests, ministers, rabbis, elders and imams. You must be qualified spiritually, morally, intellectually and emotionally to serve as a volunteer chaplain.[81]

As a volunteer organization, all members continue with their current employment

but meet for training and emergencies. Chaplains would continue with their own

employment, which may or may not be in a local church. The CAP is another way for

members to give back to their community and provide a vital service.

## CIVIL AVIATION AND AIRPORT CHAPLAINS

Pope John Paul II spoke at the Third European Seminar of Catholic Airport Chaplains in

Brussels in 2001. He identified four important points in the ministry of airport chaplains:

> 1. The airport is a true crossroads of humanity where people of all nations come into contact with one another at particular moments of life's journey.

> 2. The airport Chaplain, especially in the celebration of the Eucharist and in various forms of pastoral assistance, reminds travelers of God's loving presence and bears witness to the fundamental truths affecting all human life.

> 3. At a time when for various reasons many people are crossing frontiers in search for asylum and a new life, airport Chaplains can provide much needed support and understanding to those uprooted from their homes and all that is familiar to them.

---

[81] Civil Air Patrol Chaplains' Service, "Senior Member Training Program Specialty Track Study Guide," Civil Air Patrol Publication 221 (E), 10 Jan 1995. *Civil Air Patrol Web*. http://level2.cap.gov/documents/u_082503085137.pdf (10 Dec 2006).

4. Intensify the invaluable service to the gospel of charity.[82]

Ministry to the stranded, homeless, asylum seekers, and refugees can be resource intensive. The diversity issues are often greater than those found anywhere else, and the needs are complex. The chaplain's ministry also includes the flight crews and airport workers. If a plane goes down, the airport chaplain's crisis and trauma ministry is to the family members and friends who have been waiting, providing comfort, support, and guidance. Given the size of major airports and the diversity of people and needs, it is important that chaplains of all faiths work together and recruit volunteers to help with chaplaincy and social work.

Retired Air Force Chaplain (Lieutenant Colonel) David C. Southall manages the Washington Dulles International Airport chapel in Terminal B and is the senior chaplain, supervising two other chaplains. He jokes that his church has seventeen thousand members and twenty-four million visitors each year. He walks around the airport visiting with workers and travelers and provides counseling and help. Chaplain Southall estimates that seventy-five percent of his ministry is with staff, and he's a common site in the control tower. The chapel is open 24/7 and holds Muslim services on Fridays (prayer rugs are available), Catholic services on Saturdays, and Protestant services on Sundays.[83]

---

[82] Pope John Paul II, "Catholic Airport Chaplaincy in the 21st Century," 13 May 2003. *Vatican Web.*
http://www.vatican.va/roman_curia/pontifical_councils/migrants/documents/rc_pc_migrants_doc_2003057
  Aviation_Lyon_Marchetto_en.html (4 Nov 2006).
[83] Chris Baker, "Airport Chaplain," 8 Jul 2005. *The Washington Times Web.*
http://www.washtimes.com/business/20050707-104313-8780r.htm (4 Nov 2006).

Prison ministries have been around as long as Christians have been. In Matthew 25:36 Jesus said, "I needed clothes and you clothed me, I was sick and you looked after me, I was in prison and you came to visit me." Many churches have started jail and prison ministries to help prisoners.

Like other chaplaincy ministries, a person should feel called to serve in this ministry. The correctional chaplain is a professional, endorsed by their denomination, and specially trained. They are most often employed by a city, state, or federal department/agency to serve the offenders and sometimes their families, and are available to prison staff. Chaplains provide pastoral counseling, grief and loss counseling, crisis counseling, marriage counseling, advise management of religious and spiritual issues, and coordinate volunteer activities.[84]

In the past, success in the prison chaplain's ministry was about converting as many prisoners as possible to their form of Christianity. Today, the prison population is more diverse, and in most prisons, chaplains must be sensitive to the needs of all prisoners and offer programs that support the different faiths or bring in volunteers and community resources to help.

The Federal Religious Land Use and Institutionalized Persons Act (RLUIPA) was signed into law by President Clinton in September 2000.[85] The law specifies that prisoners must be afforded religious freedom, so some chaplain felt they had became religious programs manager. This could be seen as a positive or negative depending on

---

[84] Gary Friedman, "Chaplaincy: Facing New and Old Challenges," *Correctional Chaplain's Web.* http://www.correctionalchaplains.org/Garys%20Article/garytext.html (17 Oct 2006).
[85] Religious Land Use and Institutionalized Persons Act, "Background," *RLUIPA.com.* http://www.rluipa.com/ (12 Oct 2006).

what the circumstances are. The following excerpt shows how the act protected the

religious freedom of prisoners in California:

> Denial of Religious Materials Violates RLUIPA, First Amendment: September 28, 2006.

> California Prisoners who had been denied access to a bible and other free religious materials finally won their legal battle when the U.S. District Court for the Eastern District of California ruled that the California Department of Corrections and Rehabilitations had violated the prisoners' religious rights under the first amendment and RLUIPA.

> Jesus Christ Prison Ministries (JCPM) is a not-for-profit religious organization that provides religious materials free of charge to incarcerated persons who specifically request them. The policy of the California State Substance Abuse Treatment Facility was such that prisoners could only receive literature from a small list of "approved" commercial vendors like Amazon.com. Under this policy, state prisoners Daniel Leffel, Marvin Salinas and Daniel Marchy were not allowed to receive any of the religious materials offered by JCPM and similar non-profit religious organizations, including softbound books (bibles), unbound study guides and pamphlets or sermons and Christian music on audio tapes and compact discs. The court held that this policy violated the prisoner's free exercise of religion under RLUIPA:

> Being denied access to these religious materials compels inaction with respect to studying the Bible, listening to sermons and Christian music and propagating and teaching others about the Christian faith, all of which the undisputed evidence establishes as core elements of plaintiffs' Christian faith. Thus, the undisputed evidence demonstrates that the restrictions imposed by the authorized vendor policy place a substantial burden on the exercise of plaintiffs' religious beliefs. The case is Jesus Christ Prison Ministry v. California Department of Corrections, No. S-05-0440, 2006 WL 2792823 (E.D.Cal. Sep 28, 2006).[86]

Harsher sentences and longer sentences mean that there are now more people in

prison than ever before. Legislation requires that prison healthcare be the same as

community healthcare. Because the inmate population is getting older, there are now

prison hospices for terminally ill prisoner patients. In an effort to show compassion,

---

[86] Religious Land Use and Institutionalized Persons Act, "Denial of Religious Materials Violates RLUIPA, First Amendment," *RLUIPA.com.* Religious Land Use and Institutionalized Persons Act. "Denial of Religious Materials Violates RLUIPA, First Amendment." *RLUIPA.com.* http://www.rluipa.com/index.php/topic/20.htm?PHPSESSID=de867d8e5d9ae142025a61b8ac62e4d9 (12 Oct 2006).

empathy, support, and forgiveness, the prison hospice movement is growing and expanding and is being modeled after hospices in the community. The hospice patients get holistic care from a caring medical staff, social worker, chaplain, and volunteers from inside and outside the prison. There is also a program called, *Compassionate Release*, where terminally ill patients who qualify can go home to die.[87]

The leadership challenges of this ministry are unique. The staff is under a lot of stress and occasionally great fear, and the prisoners, at times, seem to have more rights and privileges than ever before. As an integral part of the prison staff, chaplains are concerned about the spiritual well-being of the inmates, and their eventual successful transfer back into society. If the chaplain can help them grow and mature religiously and spiritually, everyone benefits.

---

[87] Barbara Head, "The Transforming Power of Prison Hospice: Changing the Culture of Incarceration One Life at a Time," *JHPN* 7 (2005): 354-9.

# FIRE AND EMERGENCY CHAPLAINS

Fire and emergency chaplains provide fire fighters, emergency medical team staff, and their families with aid and comfort.[88] Fire chaplains serve those who serve, and on the location of a fire, they provide comfort and relief in any way possible behind the lines. The victims of fire suffer from great losses, especially if lives are lost, people and animals are burned, and possessions are destroyed. Their lives are irrevocably changed. The presence and work of chaplains in this desperate time is invaluable.

Fire fighters and emergency technicians see many horrific things in the course of their duties and careers. Many suffer from some level of post-traumatic stress disorder (PTSD), mental and physical health issues, and complicated grief and loss issues. Those who work in large cities see more *things* in one month that some see in smaller communities all year.

Chaplains must be experienced crisis and trauma counselors to meet the needs of the staff, and the victims they will encounter. Critical Incident Stress Management (CISM) training is often required for fire and emergency chaplains (also required of Red Cross chaplains). The chaplain helps the firefighters not take home some of the things they've seen and experienced, assuring them that they performed to the best of their ability, whatever the outcome. Members of the Federation of Fire Chaplains can attend the Fire Chaplain Institute which provides classes in a variety of subjects to make their chaplaincy ministry more effective.

On September 11, 2001, one of the first people on the scene of the disaster at the World Trade Center was Chaplain Michael Judge, a Franciscan Catholic priest of the

---

[88] Federation of Fire Department Chaplains. *Fire Chaplains Web.* http://www.firechaplains.org (12 Oct 2006).

New York Fire Department. Below the tower he found the triage site that had been hastily set up and began ministering to the wounded and dying firefighters. While giving the last rites to a critically injured fire fighter, he was struck by falling debris and killed.[89]

## HEALTHCARE CHAPLAINS

Healthcare chaplains are concerned with suffering and sick people and want to help them find healing. They minister to patients, families, and staff, and bring to bear multiple skills, spirituality, religion, and faith resources in the crisis of illness, critical decision-making, and ethical situations.

In healthcare, there are different chaplain positions, and although some of these look the same, there are fundamental differences: The hospital chaplain, children's hospital chaplain, hospice chaplain, prison hospice chaplain, skilled nursing facility chaplain, mental illness facility chaplain all minister to different patients, who have different yet similar needs.

### HOSPITAL CHAPLAINCY

Hospital chaplaincy is about helping people who are ill in a healthcare facility, however high-tech or humble. In the hospital, the chaplain is available to all people regardless of their beliefs and circumstances.[90] The common thread is suffering, which brings the chaplain and patient together.

Suffering brings them together, because often the chaplain has a *need* to help others, which springs from a place in their soul. Something in the chaplain's past speaks

---

[89] Donald M. Bishop, "Six Chaplains, One Faith," Nov 2001, *The Embassy of the United States of America in Nigeria Web*. http://abuja.usembassy.gov/wwwhxrdnov10.html (14 Nov 2006).
[90] Ronald Mack, Sr., *The Basics of Hospital Chaplaincy*, (Longwood, FL: Xulon Press, 2003), xi.

to their ministry in the present, perhaps from childhood hurts or blessings, and it is an area worth self-exploration. In psychological terms, this is called *countertransference*: when the chaplain's repressed feelings are aroused by the patient's suffering, emotions, and feelings. We give something of ourselves to the patient in ministry, and they give something back to us that speaks to our need to help them.[91] As CPE peers and supervisors assist a person in ministry reflection and analysis, the chaplain-in-training may discover repressed feelings that impact their ministry to suffering people, and the CPE forum can become the vehicle of the self-exploration, self-examination.

Life hurts and is full of pain. Emotional, spiritual, and physical pain follow us all through life. It separates us and brings us together. It causes us to look upward to a higher being, inward at ourselves, and outward at the world and our relationships, and informs and feeds our fears, hopes, and dreams. In the hospital, many of these issues come together, perhaps come to a head, as the patient struggles with the circumstances of illness and suffering and fear. The physical problem that brought a person to the hospital often reveals hidden emotional and spiritual issues. The person's relationships, coping, and attitudes are all closely interwoven, interconnected.

When the chaplain encounters this person, they are not trying to *fix* a patient's problems. A life has been lived, and it can be very complex. So the first thing a chaplain has to do, must do, is stop and listen. Hear their story. Professor James Gibson says, "Put on big ears."

The Reverend Walter Moczynski talks about the spiritual care ministry at Dana-Farber Cancer Institute of Boston, which is affiliated with Harvard Medical School.

---

[91] James Hillman, *In Search: Psychology and Religion* (3d ed.; Woodstock, CT: Spring Publications, 1994), 17.

"Our job is to meet the various spiritual, religious, and/or emotional needs of the patients, their families, and staff-that covers a wide range of possibilities," says Rev. Walter Moczynski, M.T.S., M.Div., Director of Pastoral Care at Dana-Farber. "We listen to people's stories and offer them counsel or support and a personal presence when desired." Chaplains offer an extensive list of services, from providing a prayer rug or rosaries to supporting a family through an ethical dilemma. "Availability, flexibility, and openness are the keys to having an effective pastoral care department," Moczynski says. "A diagnosis of cancer brings on a lot of questions: Why me? Is this a punishment? Is this a test? It can turn a person's life upside down. People with cancer need someone they can trust to talk with about these spiritual and emotional questions. . . . As patients and their families search, they need to talk with someone who respects their belief system. . . . Chaplains are available to speak with people whatever their faith or philosophical outlook on life," Moczynski says. "We don't proselytize or convert. We try to be with the patient and have an open dialogue and walk with them as far as we can on their challenging journey."[92]

Pastoral authority meets people in their expectations. Most Christian patients understand that the chaplain represents clergy, whether the chaplain actually is clergy or not. This expectation, based on the patient's religious and church experience of what a pastor is and what a pastor does, opens them up to the ministry of presence, prayer, and conversation. People who believe in prayer appreciate this intervention and tell me afterwards that they feel better, more hopeful, and less anxious.

When I get a note that a patient wants prayer before surgery, I have found that they almost eagerly await my arrival. Before praying, we introduce ourselves, meet family members if present, talk about what brought them to the hospital, and how they are feeling and coping. Touch is very important, and I often take their hand, if they are comfortable with this. If the patient and family members want, we will all hold hands to pray. We pray for a successful outcome; that God guides the doctors and nurses; that they heal quickly, and have a swift recovery. We thank God for the blessings of this day and

---

[92] Dana-Farber Medical Center, "Pastoral Care Staff," *Dana-Farber Medical Center Web.* http://www.dana-farber.org/pat/support/pastoral-care/chaplains.asp (7 Nov 2006).

for bringing about healing here in this place. Finally, we pray for family members and friends, that they are comforted in their worries and anxiety.

In the section, *Chaplains at Work*, I go into more detail about some of the challenges encountered in this ministry. On my first day in Oncology, when I walked in to visit my very first patient, she asked her family to leave so she could talk to me privately. As I sat by her side, Jean took my hand and asked me for permission to die. Her disease had progressed to a point where she was not going to be leaving the hospital, and the doctors could do no more for her. We talked about what she believed about life after death. She had made peace with God, her family, and herself, and she was ready to die. After a long talk, I did give her permission to die.

I also learned that she was on a medication for hallucinations. Her aunt shared with me that Jean only saw visions of her favorite uncle and brother who had died, nothing else. I shared this with the staff, telling them I thought Jean was in a transition phase of her life, and the doctor stopped the medication.[93] Jean and I met almost every day for a week, and then she died.

Every hospital chaplain has stories like this. In the book, *Hospital Chaplain*, Ken Mitchell describes his typical day and the many ways he is pulled from one ministry experience to another, helping patients, families, and staff.[94] Hospital chaplaincy can be dynamic, challenging, a little crazy at times, and very, very fulfilling.

Veteran Administration (VA) hospitals also have chaplains. Clergy with a military background can be very effective in ministry to retired military patients, as they might have shared similar duties and know the language. If they have been to war and

---

[93] Maggie Callanan and Patricia Kelley, *Final Gifts: Understanding the Special Awareness, Needs, and Communications of the Dying*, (New York: Bantam Books, 1997), 185.
[94] Kenneth R. Mitchell, *Hospital Chaplain* (Philadelphia: Westminster Press, 1972).

share that bond, it can make the ministry more effective. Some VA hospitals have hospice facilities and many have long-term care facilities for the aged and mentally ill.

## HOSPICE CHAPLAINCY

Hospice recognizes dying as part of the normal process of living and focuses on maintaining the quality of the remaining life. Hospice affirms life and neither hastens nor postpones death. Hospice exists in the hope and belief that through appropriate care, and the promotion of a caring community sensitive to their needs, patients and their families may be free to attain a degree of mental and spiritual preparation for death that is satisfactory to them. At the core of hospice is the belief that each person should be able to die pain free and with dignity.

Elisabeth Kübler-Ross called death *the final stage of growth*.[95] She pioneered the study of death and dying and was able to describe the stages of grief that people often experience when confronted with the news of their terminal illness: Shock, denial, anger, depression, bargaining, acceptance, and decathexis are the seven stages of dying, but people are very different, and they may go through them in different order, or bypass some stages completely. (*Decathect*: "To withdraw one's feelings of attachment from a person, idea, or object, as in anticipation of a future loss."[96] In hospice, some patients wean themselves, consciously or unconsciously, from relationships in the world when very close to death). Sometimes a person of great faith, not necessarily Christian, can hear the news of a terminal illness and go right to acceptance. Elisabeth said, "Truly

---

[95] Elisabeth Kübler-Ross, *Death: The Final Stage of Growth* (Englewood Cliffs, NJ: Prentice-Hall, 1975), 145.

[96] Dictionary.com, "Decathect," (Based on the Random House Unabridged Dictionary, © Random House, Inc. 2006. Dictionary.com Unabridged v 1.0.1.). http://dictionary.reference.com/browse/decathect (3 Nov 2006).

religious people with a deep abiding relationship with God have found it much easier to face death with equanimity. . . . Religious people also go through the same stages of dying, but quicker and with less turmoil."[97]

Terminally ill patients have special needs, which they are willing to share if the chaplain takes the time to listen. Being fully present and attentive, willing to enter into their world without judgment, fear, or anxiety, can be very reassuring to them. It allows them to open up with those things that might be bothering them.[98] As a hospice chaplain, I found that it was often easier for the person to open up to me than to family members; partly because I was a stranger, but also because I would just hold their hand and listen.

In this conversation, we hear their feelings, and we learn what is important, what is not important, what gives meaning at this stage of life, and if there is unfinished business, regrets, worries, or guilt. I find this stage of life to be filled with great authenticity: thanatological authenticity. When confronted with their mortality, a lot of the posturing and pretense of life, and those many walls we have built around us for protection, come crumbling down. In this place, people want to *clear the air*, talk about what they feel is most important, and find reconciliation, forgiveness, hope, and emotional and spiritual well-being. These can be conversations of great depth and meaning. This is sacred ground.

Generally, people don't take the time to hear another person's story, especially the complete story. But people often want to tell the story of their life; their journey, loves, losses, successes, failures, the heights and depths, the places they've lived, and what and who was important. Just taking the time to sit with them and hear their story can be a

---

[97] Elisabeth Kübler-Ross, *Questions & Answers on Death and Dying: A companion volume to On Death and Dying* (New York: Touchstone, 1974), 163.
[98] Virginia Morris, *Talking About Death*, (Chapel Hill, NC: Algonquin Books, 2001), passim.

very valuable gift to them in their closing days. "I want you to hear about me–a person who mattered."

Sometimes there's a sense of urgency. When that happens, I find that the patient goes right to the heart of their thoughts and feelings about things. I find this very refreshing. Discussions about beliefs, suffering, God, fairness, life after death, meaning, spirituality, religion, prayer, burdens, existence, purpose, relationships, and many other things percolate to the surface.

There are times when words are not appropriate. The patient is at peace with their situation and has accepted their illness, and they are not particularly interested in activity or conversation. What they do appreciate is the presence: the quiet reassuring presence, holding a hand, perhaps soft singing, quiet reading of poetry or bible passages. Silence, in these moments, can be a gift: listening to the wind in the eaves, or the distant bark of a dog, watching the bird at the feeder. In our silence, we let them know it is okay to be silent. In our comfort, we let them know we are not uncomfortable in the silence, and enjoy just being with them. Touch, reassurance, and being at peace are the ministry of presence.[99]

In her lifetime, Elisabeth Kübler-Ross worked with many patients who were terminally ill. In her book, *Questions & Answers*, her interviewer asked, "In all your research on death, what is your personal belief on what happens after death?" She replied, "Before I started working with dying patients, I did not believe in a life after death. I now do believe in a life after death, beyond a shadow of doubt."[100]

---

[99] Kenneth C. Haugk, *Don't Sing Songs to a Heavy Heart: How to relate to those who are suffering*, (St Louis: Stephen Ministries, 2004), passim.
[100] Kübler-Ross, *Questions & Answers*, 167.

As a hospital and hospice chaplain, I have come to believe that every person who dies gets escorted: that an angel, Jesus, a spiritual being, a relative, a friend, or someone, or something comes to help them find their way into the next life. There is a period of time, a month, a week, or a few hours from death, when the dying person seems to have one foot in this world and one foot in the next-the transition phase. This experience transcends faith and religion, theology and philosophy, and believers and nonbelievers.

I believe this happens for two reasons: hope and comfort. First, hearing a dying person speak of seeing and talking to people we can't see is quite common, and I'm sure it is not a hallucination brought on by medications and declining health. These revelations bolster the hope and faith of the patient and the family, by affirming that life does not end in this world, and in the next life, we will be reunited with our loved ones. Second, at the same time, this knowledge brings great comfort to the patient, because it helps take away the fear of death and the future. For family and friends, it reminds them that death is a normal experience that all people must go through, and there is hope beyond death.

I believe dying people have these experiences because, just as all human beings share a commonality of birth, being born of a man and woman, all human beings share a common experience of death. All I am speaking about is the actual dying experience; I am not speculating on what happens in the escorting event itself, where people might go, or what else might happen afterwards. Different religions and faiths believe different things, and some people don't believe anything at all. Yet, I've had patients who were devout atheists, who saw spiritual beings and talked to them, and their experience became a source of rich discussion.

Several people have told me they just didn't believe these stories, mostly because they already had their own beliefs about what happens to people at death: the body and soul sleep until the resurrection. To believe these stories puts there belief in question or possibly changes it completely.

First, these stories are like the stories we hear from children. They are absolutely genuine and borne out of the innocence of unusual and sacred encounters. Who can question the child that wakes up from a coma and tells stories of angels who came to visit with them? Or, the child who miraculously survives a drowning in a pool, to tell stories about how an angel came and sat with them until they recovered. Likewise, the people who see and talk to relatives who have died and angels on their death bed have nothing to prove and nothing to gain. This is especially true for the atheists I mentioned.

Second, to believe that the body and soul only sleep is in contradiction with the Bible. A good example of what I'm speaking of here is what happened to Jesus. He was crucified and died, and his body was placed in a new tomb.[101] Yet, we also know that he went to hell and preached to the people in captivity.[102] On the third day, he resurrected with all of them and joined with his body.[103] His body was asleep, and his soul was somewhere else. The Apostle Paul said it this way, "We are confident, I say, and willing rather to be absent from the body, and to be present with the Lord."[104] Yes, the body sleeps until the resurrection, but we, ourselves, are in a heavenly place of some kind. I'm not saying it is "the heaven," the final destination, and I'm not saying that it is the same for everyone. But we get escorted by someone to a place.

---

[101] Matt 27:57-60.
[102] 1 Peter 3:18-22.
[103] Matt 27: 52-53.
[104] 2 Cor 5:8, *KJV*.

I also don't understand the significance of being reunited at a later date with a body that in many cases has been reduced into the basic elements of the earth. For some reason, the resurrection event seems to be important in the Bible, because a lot of emphasis is placed on this spiritual and physical reuniting.

There are many books about near-death experiences, and I am not talking about that here, and I am not suggesting anything related to mysticism or cosmic consciousness. I am just reporting what my patients experienced, how it blessed me and those around them, and seemed quite normal given the circumstances.

In the book, *Final Gifts*, the authors, Maggie Callanan and Patricia Kelley, recorded the stories of hospice patients and have categorized them based on their experiences. They have a chapter on *Nearing Death Awareness*, which is broken down into such chapters as, *Being in the Presence of Someone Not Alive: "I'm Not Alone;"* *Seeing a Place: "I See Where I'm Going;"* and many more. My point is that this is common among dying people.

> Recognize the differences that distinguish Nearing Death Awareness from near-death experiences. Patients with Nearing Death Awareness are not clinically dead, often have such experiences over time and in a more gradual way, and usually can talk during the experiences, making them able to share these insights with others. You can help them in their struggles to share this information, and can learn from them as well.[105]

In the last chapter of *Final Gifts*, they talk about how to be with someone who is having these experiences with some practical guidelines. Here are a few:

> Accept and validate what the dying person tells you. If he says, "I see a beautiful place!" say, "I'm so please. I can see that it makes you happy," or "I'm so glad you're telling me this. I really want to understand what's happening to you. Can you tell me more?"

---

[105] Callanan, *Final Gifts*, 230.

Don't argue or challenge. By saying something like "You couldn't possibly have seen Mother, she's been dead for ten years," you could increase the dying person's frustration and isolation, and run the risk of putting an end to further attempts at communication.

If you don't know what to say, don't say anything. Sometimes the best response is simply to touch the dying person's hand, or smile and stroke his or her forehead. Touching give the very important message, "I'm with you." Or you could say, "That's interesting, let me think about it."

Remember that sometimes the one dying picks an unlikely confident [the chaplain]. Dying people often try to communicate important information to someone who makes them feel safe-who won't get upset or be taken aback by such confidences. If you're an outsider chosen for this role, share the information as gently and completely as possible with the appropriate family members or friends [and facility staff, if not at home]. They may be more familiar with innuendos in a message because they know the person well.[106]

Being with people as they near death, and being the person who helps them in that experience, can be one of the most rewarding experiences as a chaplain, and in life.

## CERTIFICATION

Many hospitals and hospices employ professional chaplains to assist with the spiritual needs of patients, families, and staff. The Joint Commission on the Accreditation of Hospital Organizations certifies hospitals. JCAHO requires that hospital chaplains (and those hospice agencies affiliated with hospitals) be trained through the Association for Clinical Pastoral Education (CPE) and certified by one of the following organizations: International Chaplains Association (ICA), the Association of Professional Chaplains (APC), the National Association of Catholic Chaplains (NACC), or the National Association of Jewish Chaplains (NAJC). In Canada chaplains may be certified by the Canadian Association for Pastoral Practice and Education (CAPPE).

---

[106] Callanan, *Final Gifts*, 226-8.

Certification typically requires a Master of Divinity degree, faith group ordination or commissioning, faith group endorsement, and four units of Clinical Pastoral Education. The NACC has provisions for lay chaplain candidates due to a chronic shortage of Catholic priests to serve as chaplains.

Membership in the Association of Professional Chaplains has many benefits, and first on the list is, "Professional standing and recognition of competence as a board certified chaplain in a professional society with established national standards including a code of professional ethics."[107] One theme that runs through these certification groups is the word *professional*. I believe it is important to be a member of a national professional association of peers, with accountability, resources, professional development, education, networking, and partnership and leadership opportunities.

## HEALTHCARE CHAPLAINCY DYNAMICS

All illness impacts human development with spiritual and emotional components. Likewise, the practice of chaplain care meets people in their spiritual and emotional needs. I am careful to understand and say that the chaplain *meets* people, instead of saying that the chaplain fixes things, or makes clever suggestions, or has any miraculous answers.

This was particularly painful to me when I encountered the young family who had lost a baby. It was imperative that I not try to give them coy or religious answers. All I could give them was a heartfelt, *I am so sorry*, and listen empathetically to the story of their heartache and loss.

---

[107] Association of Professional Chaplains, "Membership Offers Valuable Benefits," *Healing Spirit* 1 (2006): 34.

I firmly believe in the spiritual dimension being the essential part of an person's striving for health, wholeness, and meaning in life. The spiritual dimension is understood in relationships, and I seek to hear the patient's story and their understanding of those relationships in their lives, as a way of ministering to them.

## JEWISH CHAPLAINS

In the Old Testament, it could be argued that references to priests working with the army were early examples of Jewish chaplains. Jewish clergy have been involved as chaplains in all aspects of society, including the military, where they have died in ministry for their country. Chaplains have ministered on the battlefields and in the hospitals to help young men in their hour of greatest need. I pointed out earlier that the Civil War was the advent of modern chaplaincy, and that was no more true than for the Jewish chaplains.

Rabbi Daniel D. Stuhlman spoke about being a Jewish chaplain and described the origins of professional Jewish chaplaincy, which started during the Civil War:

> Jewish chaplaincy as a profession started with the military. . . .In July-August of 1861, Congress passed legislation to appoint chaplains to the Army. Thousands of Jews had volunteered for both the Union and Confederacy. The legislation stated that the chaplains had to a member of a Christian denomination. Members of Congress and the Jewish community were split as to whether this was discrimination or not. Dr Isaac Meyer Wise, who opposed the war, at first did very little about changing the legislation, but later in cooperation with Ohio representative Clement L. Vallandigham, fought to have the legislation changed on the basis that rabbis and priests can be just as good citizens of this country. Dr Arnold Fischel was appointed to lobby for Jewish representation in the chaplaincy. On March 12, 1862, the Senate passed legislation that abolished discrimination; however the House delayed passage for a few months. The bill became law on July 17, 1862.[108]

---

[108] Daniel D. Stuhlman, Daniel D, "Librarian's Lobby," Feb 2005, *Stuhlman Personal Web.* http://home.earthlink.net/~ddstuhlman/crc80.htm (14 Nov 2006).

Rabbi Stuhlman went on to speak about being a Jewish hospital chaplain, and much of what he said pertained to all chaplains, but in the following piece he touched on several aspects unique to Jewish chaplaincy ministry:

> The era of professional, full-time trained [Jewish] hospital chaplains is about 55 years old. The mitzvah of *bikur holim* (visiting the sick) was given to all Jews. We are required to help the patient to the best of our ability. . . . Chaplains may also help in time of a *simha* such as help arranging for a *brit milah* for a baby born in the hospital. They may arrange for kosher food, Hanukah lights, meditation therapy, music therapy or other non-medical help. Chaplains have the connections to hospital administrations and religious communities along with the training so that they can serve the needs of the patients, their families and the medical staff.[109]

In a magazine interview, Chaplain Rabbi Martin Scharf of Kivel Care Center in Phoenix, Arizona, candidly spoke about his CPE training, what chaplaincy was like in the hospital, and how it affected him personally. In the following paragraph, he talks about how he ministered to a man who was afraid of dying:

> Once a psychiatrist, a Jew, asked me if he's going to heaven. He hadn't gone to synagogue in over 40 years, even though his own father (prayed) three times a day. So I said to him, "How many people did you help as a psychiatrist?" He thought about it and finally admitted that he had helped many, many people. So I said to him, "The Talmud says, if you save one life, it's as if you've saved the whole world," said Eisenbach. "I remind them of their accomplishments. They don't need me to tell them they're going to die; they already know that. I'm just there to listen, tell them their life was worthwhile, and validate their pain."[110]

A Buddhist teacher tells the story of a young Jewish woman who came from Israel to a meditation center in the United States and was worried about how to integrate her meditation with her Jewish beliefs. The Buddhist teacher told her how to incorporate the meditation into her Jewish heritage and practices:

---

[109] Stuhlman, "Librarian's Lobby."
[110] Abigail Pickus, "Jewish Chaplains Offer Spiritual Guidance," 1 Oct 1999, *Jewish News of Greater Phoenix Web*. http://www.jewishaz.com/jewishnews/991001/chaplain.shtml (14 Nov 2006).

A Jewish girl from Israel came to meditate. She felt happy and calm in meditation, but she was worried. She said, "I do not want to forget my heritage. I was born in Jerusalem and am steeped in Jewish tradition." I answered her: "No problem. When you finish meditating, say the *Shmah*!" This is the ancient prayer of the Jews to be said each morning of their lives and on their deathbeds. It consists of the words, "Hear, O Israel, the Lord our God, the Lord is one." This, to those of the Jewish faith, may be a solacing thought, one that may yield them comfort, I told her.[111]

There is a chronic shortage of Jewish chaplains in the military. The Jewish Welfare Board (JWB) Chaplains' Committee, founded during World War I, works to encourage rabbis to join the military and Veteran Affairs medical centers as chaplains to Jewish men and women around the world. The JWBCC provide all kinds of support, training, and information for chaplains and volunteers. Rabbi Harold Robinson is the chairman of the JWB Chaplains' Council and visited the Horn of Africa during a Jewish holiday. His story below, speaks to the needs of Jewish men and women stationed overseas:

> "Nothing would bring them together without the catalyst of a JWB rabbi," said Rabbi Harold Robinson about Jews in the military when he returned from his High Holiday trip to the Horn of Africa. JWB rabbis, both active and reserve, and from every military branch, were all over the Mid East Area of operations, including Afghanistan, Bahrain, Kuwait, and Iraq. Robinson, the director of JWB Jewish Chaplains' Council, went to bring a sense of the *Yom Tov* to Jewish military personnel and contractors stationed in Djibouti, the former French Somalia, at the mouth of the Red Sea. The Jews stationed there would each have been alone otherwise, and said, "Jews are hungry for their moment to be Jewish and Jewish chaplains create little bubbles of time." In Robinson's experience as a Navy chaplain, a military base begins to program when it learns that a rabbi is planning a visit. The Jews in the area, who feel a Jewish loneliness, come when there's a reason to come. So a Jewish chaplain is a stimulus to action in several different ways.[112]

Jewish women chaplains are mentioned in the section on *Women in Chaplaincy*.

---

[111] Figen, "Is Buddhism a Religion?"
[112] Harold L. Robinson, "JWB Chaplains Bring Holiday to the Troops," *JWBCC Web*. http://www.jcca.org/jwb/ (16 Aug 2006).

## LAW ENFORCEMENT CHAPLAINS

Law enforcement chaplains serve local police, highway patrol, the Federal Bureau of

Investigations, the department of Alcohol, Tobacco and Firearms, and many others. Law

enforcement chaplains are present at the moment of crisis and must minister effectively

to the police and the victims. They do not interfere with the duties of the police, but are

available if called to assist or help in the realm of their professional expertise. These

chaplains provide police and victims with counseling, comfort, and presence in

extraordinary circumstances. Incidents that cause stressful emotional highs and lows, and

physical, mental, and spiritual anguish, all combine to create burdens many people find

hard, if not impossible, to carry. In moments of danger and confusion, the chaplain in law

enforcement, like the military chaplain, can be an island of calm and hope.

The following excerpt from the International Conference of Police Chaplains,

gives us a little insight into the scope of their ministry:

Police officers often say to us that "I wouldn't do the difficult work you do for anything!" They are trained and able to face armed robbers or control an unruly crowd. But a sobbing parent at a SIDS (sudden infant death syndrome) incident can erase even the most stoic officer's composure. Entering that saddest of moments is no easier for a chaplain, but the chaplain brings experience, training, and skills to the tragedy that are as specialized as the law enforcement resources every officer develops with training and experience. As a team, both chaplain and officer make an important difference in the lives of persons touched by tragedy. We work together."[113]

The police chaplain's duties are many and varied. The following list outlines

many of the things that law enforcement chaplains do:

Law enforcement chaplains do some or all of the following: Counsel law enforcement officers, counsel other members of a department, counsel the families of law enforcement officers and other department personnel, visit sick or injured officers and departmental personnel in homes and hospitals, make death notifications, provide assistance to victims, teach officers in areas such as Stress Management, Ethics, Family Life, and Pre-retirement classes and courses, serve as part of a department's Crisis Response Team, assist at suicide incidents, serve as liaison with other clergy in the community, provide for the spiritual needs of prisoners, furnish expert responses to religious questions, offer prayers at special occasions such as recruit graduations, awards ceremonies, and dedication of buildings, serve on review boards, award boards, and other committees, and deal with transients and the homeless.[114]

Like fire chaplains, police chaplains serve those who serve the community. Many

clergy are volunteer fire and police chaplains. They may learn the skills needed on the

job, but continued education will only make them more effective in their ministry.

Regional training opportunities are listed on the ICPC website (see Appendix A).

Most chaplains working in large, active chaplaincy programs will see more trauma in one year than most law enforcement officers will see in their careers. So the "costs" you are going to pay and the "consequences" you are going to realize by working full-time in an agency of this scope have to be contemplated. Saturation and accumulated trauma of this magnitude can lead to burn-out,

---

[113] International Conference of Police Chaplains, "Chaplains at Work," *ICPC4COPS.org.* http://www.icpc4cops.org/ (20 Oct 2006).
[114] Police Chaplains, "Chaplain's at Work."

compassion fatigue, vicarious traumatization, or secondary traumatic stress-all potentially career ending issues.[115]

Self-care is very important to maintaining good mental and spiritual health. Without a good self-care routine, this ministry would be limited to a few years, at most. The section on self-care talks about different ways chaplains can care for themselves and continue in ministry.

## MENTAL HEALTH CHAPLAINS

Despite the fact that nearly ten percent of people are affected by serious mental illness, there is still a stigma in society. The person who walks by on the street talking loudly to no one is usually ignored, because they are probably homeless, penniless, and different. If they are perceived to be a danger to themselves and society, they might be put in an institution. At one time, mental illness was something a family was embarrassed about and tried to hide, but bipolar disorder, depression, schizophrenia, and increased incidents of Post-Traumatic Stress Disorder are more common in society. In addition, people born with developmental disabilities, substance abuse neurological degeneration, chemical imbalances, and head injuries are all lumped together as mentally ill and often shunned by society. These people are suffering from both an illness or injury, and a community that seldom understands and rejects them out of fear and misunderstanding.

The mental health chaplain seeks to come alongside these people in their struggle and help them reestablish broken relationships, regain those things they have lost, and build their faith. The chaplain's ministry may take them to the streets of the city, seeking those disenfranchised by the world, the mental health unit in a hospital, or the mental

---

[115] Chuck Lorrain, "Costs & Consequences: What is the price of full-time chaplaincy?" *International Conference of Police Chaplains Web.* http://www.icpc4cops.org/ (20 Oct 2006).

health institution. Mentally ill people are often in a confused state and not likely to seek help or know that help is available, so the chaplain becomes like the shepherd looking for the lost sheep. People with feelings of hopelessness, shame, fear, hurt and mistrust need a person who is not afraid of them, who is willing to help them find healing, a stable place in society, and self-worth. The chaplain works closely with churches, community outreach services, volunteers, social workers and medical teams, and when possible educates people and groups, so they learn about mental illness and how they can help bring love and caregiving to these vulnerable and broken people. The definition of spirituality encompasses all relationships, which means the mentally ill person's struggle is not only with the brain disorder, but is also a suffering of the soul. The chaplain helps bring spiritual care, love, healing, comfort, hope, companionship, and the assurance of God's love and forgiveness to people in suffering and in desperate need of soul care.

When I worked on the mental health unit at the hospital, I learned that these were normal people in great need and desperate suffering. Some had chemical imbalances, or were overtaken by the stresses and horrors of life, or born with disabilities, and others had abused some kind of drug until their brains were damaged. Many people suffered from unresolved griefs and losses, chronic anxiety, loss of hope, fear of people, God, life, and a deteriorating ability to cope. My heart went out to them and the staff who worked there, and I found that if you were fully present, listening, hearing and encouraging as they told their story, it gave them a glimmer of hope. They knew someone did care and wanted them to find healing and wholeness.

Mental illness is not like a broken leg. The brain is incredibly complex and when it is not working properly, doctors can help bring some normalization, but a cure might not be possible. That in itself might be a little depressing, because it means that a person might need to manage medications with poor side effects, if they want to minimize symptoms and function with a semblance of normality in society. The community gives them a precious gift, when they accept the differences of the mentally challenged and mentally ill people, and just bring them with love into the family.

"I was a stranger and you invited me in, I needed clothes and you clothed me, I was [mentally] sick and you looked after me. The King will reply, 'I tell you the truth, whatever you did for one of the least of these brothers of mine, you did for me.' "[116] Perhaps, just knowing about the need will lead some people to look more closely at the mentally ill in their communities.

## MILITARY CHAPLAINS

The first part of this study was about military history and the work of chaplains in that ministry. As long as the military is required, there will be chaplains. Chaplains are in the active military, which consists of four branches (Army, Air Force, Navy, and Coast Guard), the National Guard units in each state (Army, Air Force, and Naval Militia), and the Reserves (Army, Air Force, and Navy). The active duty military and the Reserves answer to the President of the United States. The National Guard answers to the Governor of the state to which they belong. The Reserves are made up of people who either served previously on active duty, or joined the Reserves directly. Reservists are there to support the active duty military, should they need more people. Traditionally, the Reservists seldom saw action, but in recent years, they have been deployed to Iraq in support of that conflict, along with many National Guard units.

---

[116] Matt 25:35b-36, 40.

Although each branch of the military has their own chaplain school, chaplains are officers and the requirements for duty and commissioning are the same for all officers. The major differences revolve around the branches of service (Army, Air Force, Navy, and Coast Guard) and how their people and equipment are deployed. Given the many possibilities, the requirements for chaplains are often open and ongoing. There is a chronic shortage of Catholic and Jewish Chaplains, and those people interested in this ministry should see a local recruiter of the branch that interests them to find out what denominations are needed.

During times of war, the requirements are higher, and after wars there is always a time of downsizing, when chaplains might find themselves in Reserve or National Guard units, or decommissioned and returned to civilian life. In the Reserves and National Guard, a clergy person could continue to have a church ministry and serve on weekends and two weeks during the summer.

The pay and retirement are good, but like all officers in the military, some moving around is required. Special assignments might require special training, and chaplains who want to be with Infantry units might find themselves camping a lot, jumping out of airplanes, and hiking in all kinds of weather and terrain. Chaplains in the Navy might be stationed at a naval base, but everyone has to do time at sea. Cruises can be for a few months, six months, or even a year depending on mission requirements. Military chaplains can also serve at military prisons.

The Antiochian Orthodox Church provides guidelines for priests and clergy who are considering a position as a military chaplain. I've included a few of those guidelines

# MUSLIM CHAPLAINS

After the attack on the World Trade Center September 11, 2001 one of the first people to wade into the fray to help, was Imam Izak-El Mu'eed Pasha, chaplain to the New York Police Department since 1999. Imam Pasha worked tirelessly to help, console, and heal everyone suffering from the destruction. The Imam of a Harlem mosque, he was highly respected for his work in the community bringing together people divided by their many differences. So it was not unusual to find him on the podium at Yankee Stadium two weeks later, as the community came together to grieve their losses. People wept openly as he spoke:

> Imam Pasha came to the stage. His voice told his sorrow and his anguish. "We, Muslims, Americans, stand today with a heavy weight on our shoulder that those who would dare to do such dastardly acts claim our faith. They are no believers in God at all. Nor do they believe in His messenger Muhammad, prayers and peace be upon Him. We condemn their acts, their cowardly acts, and we stand with our country against all that would come against us. We are members of one human family, one human dignity, one human worth. That worth that God has given to us, the goodness that He has created us in, no single group or nation will be able to destroy that. We are one with the Creator of the heavens and the earth. We are one with members of faith, both Jewish, Christian, and others here today and those who are absent. We are believers."[118]

At the close of his speech, he read from the Surah, *Time Through Ages*, and prayed:

> By the time verily mankind is in loss, except such as have faith and do righteous deeds and join together in the mutual enjoining of truth and of patience and consistency. May God guide us. May God bless our mayor, our governor, and our president and all of you. Do not allow the ignorance of people to have you attack your good neighbor. We are Muslims, but we are Americans. Amen.[119]

---

[118] Bishop, "Six Chaplains."
[119] ibid.

The Department of Defense started the Muslim Chaplain Corps in 1993, and as of

September, 2003, there were twelve Muslim chaplains on active duty. The Muslim Corps

has been under increasing scrutiny since September 11, 2001, because the Graduate

School for Islamic Social Sciences (GSISS), the Islamic Society of North America

(ISNA), and the American Muslim Armed Forces and Veteran Affairs Council

(AMAFVAC), who nominate Muslim clerics for military and prison chaplaincies have

been linked to the Wahhabi sect of Islam.

> Professor Ali Asani of Harvard University, author Stephen Schwartz and other experts have asserted that AMAFVAC, GSISS, and ISNA are funded generously by Saudi Arabia and hold closely to the religious tenets of the radical Wahhabi sect of Islam, Saudi Arabia's official state religion. Far from promoting a pluralist approach to the world, Wahhabi Islam is widely acknowledged to be exclusionary and extreme, denigrating not only other religions but also other forms of Islamic belief held by Shi'a and moderate Sunni Muslims.[120]

> In June 2003, the websites for the Navy and the Air Force chaplains were found to have links to Islamworld.net, a website that espouses Wahhabism, and contains links to lectures by fundamentalist clerics, some of whom advocate jihad against the United States and denigrate Christianity and Judaism as "forms of disbelief." The websites described Islamworld.net as "rich in information about the Islamic faith, including an introduction for non-Muslims" and "basics for new Muslims." After news reports publicized the extremist connection, the Air Force removed the link and the Navy issued a disclaimer saying it has no control over material published on independent web sites.[121]

Muslim chaplains who do not follow Wahhabism are still caught up in the fear

that has gripped the world in the aftermath of the many terrorist actions. But if they have

an open and inclusive ministry that seeks to help all people who are in need, their

ministry will vindicate itself in the eyes of those they work with and for.

---

[120] Robert Longley, "Terror-Linked Group May Supply Muslim US Military Chaplains," 26 Sept 2003, *U.S. Government Info Web.* http://usgovinfo.about.com/b/a/029839.htm (15 Nov 2006).
[121] Longley, "Terror-Linked Group."

# PEDIATRIC CHAPLAINCY

Pediatric Chaplaincy is about ministry to children, families, and staff. Parents are hardwired to protect their kids. Unlike other hospital and hospice chaplaincies, sick and injured children speak to our hearts and cause us to respond protectively. The anticipatory grief is not just about the possible loss of a life, it is about the possible loss of a life that could have been.

Parents are just trying to survive and make sense of what's going on. As they seek to comfort their child, they are often balancing the needs of other children, jobs, and the financial impact, all while trying to learn more about what is going on and what they can possibly do.

When the children are suffering, the parents really need the chaplain. Usually they will tell the chaplain what they need, but are not willing to go very deep in their grief, but the chaplain's symbolic presence of hope, connection, and community is reassuring.

Children seem to be more aware of things than adults give them credit for. Children have a special spirituality and faith which is genuine and authentic. When children, who do not have a religious background, speak of talking to angels, of light, and of hope, a door is cracked open, and we get a small glimpse into heaven.[122]

# SENATE AND HOUSE CHAPLAINS

The United States Senate makes it a point of distinguishing between Church and State, and God and State, by honoring the chaplaincy and endorsing its importance. The U.S. Senate and each state has a Senate Chaplain, who are nominated by a congressional

---

[122] Krusemark, Mardi, Rev., Chaplain, Pediatric Grief and Loss Care Manager, Interview 14 Nov 2006.

member and is then elected by the body and appointed by the Speaker. Different states elect chaplains for different lengths of time; anywhere from one-year terms to multiple years and multiple terms, and part-time to full-time. The House Chaplain is elected for a two-year term at the start of the Congress, but the Senate Chaplain does not have to be elected at the beginning of the term. There are also guest chaplains, of all faiths, who are invited to open daily sessions in prayer.

Although the full-time Senate Chaplain earns $140,300 per year, and the House Chaplain earns $160,600, they are allowed to continue their service in their congregation, if they so desire.[123]

The first chaplain of the U.S. Senate, elected in 1878, was the Rt. Reverend Samuel Provost, Episcopal Bishop of New York. The most famous of the U.S. Senate chaplains was the Reverend Peter Marshall, pastor of New York Avenue Presbyterian Church in Washington, D.C. He was famous for his preaching, and after his death his wife, Catherine, wrote the book, *A Man Called Peter*, which was later made into an inspirational movie.

The chaplains open each chamber of Congress with prayer. The chaplain's duties include counseling staff, consulting staff on theological and moral issues, teaching bible studies, hosting the Senate Prayer Breakfast, and facilitating small groups.

---

[123] Congressional Research Service of the Library of Congress, "House and Senate Chaplains," *U.S. Senate Web*. http://www.senate.gov/reference/resources/pdf/RS20427.pdf (22 Oct 2006).

UNIVERSITY CHAPLAINS

Universities and colleges want to be inclusive and tolerant of all faiths, beliefs, and practices, and often employ or provide a wide range of chaplains to meet the actual or potential religious and spiritual needs of the student body. The following is the list of chaplains associated with the University of Victoria, British Columbia, Canada: Anglican, Baha'i, Baptist, Buddhist, Catholic, Christian Science, Judaic, Lutheran, Muslim, Orthodox, Pentecostal, The Salvation Army, United Church of Christ, and Wiccan.[124]

University chaplaincy could be a complicated ministry for some people, but the focus should be toward like-believers, supporting them in the school environment. Students are very vulnerable, and many suffer from doubts of faith from new material they are exposed to and irreligious professors. Many suffer from depression while being away from home, family, and friends, and the many stresses of the academic life. Some students turn to alcohol, drugs, sex, and thoughtless spending, because there are few oversights, little or no adult supervision, and they throw off the restrictions and rules they grew up with. In these and many other situations, the chaplain leader can be a steady influence and a rudder for these young minds as they navigate new and uncharted waters.

At the University of Queensland, Australia, the religious body nominates a chaplain for the university position, but the university's Senate Chaplaincy Committee votes for a candidate, who is then approved or disapproved by the University Senate. The chaplains keep the Senate Chaplaincy Committee informed of their ministry, and once a year the committee sends a report on their activities to the Senate and the nominating

---

[124] University of Victoria, "Faith Groups and Interfaith Chaplains," 2006. *University of Victoria Web.* http://web.uvic.ca/interfaith/chaplains/ (18 Oct 2006).

religious body. The chaplains are allowed volunteer assistants and aides. If a religious

body wants to be recognized by the university and have a chaplain presence, they must

contact the Vice-Chancellor and Senate Chaplaincy Committee, who talk to university

chaplains, interview the spokesperson of the religious body, and then make a

recommendation to the Senate. The religious body has to committee to funding the

Chaplaincy Services. Although a chaplain may represent a specific religious

denomination, they minister in an ecumenical, multi-faith environment for the good of

all, referring students, as necessary to a chaplain of their faith. Chaplains provide pastoral

care to students and staff and are involved in many university services: children services,

issues of harassment, bullying, racism, sexual harassment, and disability issues.[125]

## WORKPLACE CHAPLAINS

Industrial and business leaders are discovering the value of workplace chaplains for the

well-being and morale of their employees. The chaplain knows the employees, and

knows about their stresses, fears, job and family concerns, and personal struggles. The

chaplain spends time with the employees in the workplace, and provides faith-based

counseling for personal problems, family issues, and substance abuse. Often a chaplain

can defuse violence in the workplace just by being present.

Marketplace Ministries of Dallas was started by Gil Stricklin, a retired Army

chaplain in 1984. He modestly says that God started the company, and he was the first

employee. Gil saw a need for a religious presence and counseling in the workplace,

where traditional employee-based psychologists and personnel director programs had

---

[125] University of Queensland, "Chaplaincy Services," 26 May 2005, *University of Queensland Web.* http://www.uq.edu.au/hupp/index.html?page=25350&pid=25347 (16 Nov 2006).

failed.[126] As of 2004, Marketplace Ministries had one thousand, two hundred chaplains

serving in thirty-five states.

Corporate Chaplains of America, in North Carolina, has fifty full-time chaplains

and many part-time chaplains serving over three hundred businesses. It is estimated that

over four thousand chaplains now serve in the workplace nationwide.[127]

The Yale Divinity School annual *National Conference on Workplace Chaplaincy*

for November 2006 scheduled talks as follows: Ministry to a multi-cultural and multi-

faith workforce; Interfaith dimensions; How we do chaplaincy in the workplace; Spiritual

foundations for chaplaincy; Entrepreneurial skills for workplace chaplains; Making the

case for workplace chaplaincy; Forum: Coalition of workplace chaplains.[128]

The following is a story about how a chaplain helped a company and an

employee:

> Aaron was a good employee. He worked in our shipping/receiving area, primarily
> third shift. He contracted cancer and fought it for a year before dying at the age of
> 26. Aaron had no family living nearby, nor was he part of a local faith
> community. When his health crisis struck, our company chaplain shared the love
> of Jesus Christ with Aaron and his family, helped them cope throughout the year,
> and provided the family with an oasis of solace after his death. We at Zion
> Industries all cared for Aaron, but it was our chaplain who spent time with him, in
> the hospital and at home. We all could share many good stories about Aaron, but
> it was our chaplain who really knew him and who performed the funeral service.
> We, as a company, made some difference in the life of an employee and his
> family, but it was our chaplain who made a lasting difference.[129]

The National Institute of Business and Industrial Chaplains certifies chaplains for

business settings in the United States.

---

[126] Tom Toolen, *Chaplains on Frontline in Corporate Wars*, The Spiritual Herald Newspaper (New York: Eastern Tsalagi Publishing Co, Aug 2004), 24.
[127] Toolen, *Chaplains on Frontline*, 24.
[128] Yale Center for Faith & Culture, "National Conference on Workplace Chaplaincy," 2006. *Yale University Web.* http://www.yale.edu/faith/esw/ncwc.htm (28 Sept 2006).
[129] Keith Starcher, "Should You Hire a Workplace Chaplain?" 2003. *Christianity Today Web.* http://www.christianitytoday.com/workplace/articles/issue8-chaplain.html (10 Sept 2006).

## MISCELLANEOUS CHAPLAIN OPPORTUNITIES

Anywhere people in need find themselves outside the traditional religious establishment, a chaplain might be found. In addition to those already mentioned, chaplains can be attached to some high schools and seminaries; retirement communities; membership clubs such as the Knights of Columbus, Eagles, Elks, Veterans of Foreign Wars, American Legion; professional sports teams, scout troops, cruise ships, and even nightclubs.

With the advent of the Homeland Security department, there is more emphasis on emergency management. With that in mind, many counties across the country now have chaplains, many in full-time paid positions, for their county emergency management offices. Go to your county employment center for information on these positions or call your county emergency management office.

The Assemblies of God church promotes chaplains in all walks of life. On their website, they list all of the places where they have placed chaplains:

> The Assemblies of God currently has chaplains ministering in jails, prisons, juvenile facilities, nursing homes, hospitals, hospice centers, truck stops, rodeos, race tracks, rescue missions, airports, law enforcement agencies, fire departments, emergency medical services, industries, businesses, schools, sports arenas, motorcycle rallies and mental health facilities. We continue to expand into new areas as God leads.[130]

The range and scope of chaplain ministry will grow as God puts the burden on a person's hearts to take ministry outside the church to meet others in their own environment and with their own unique needs.

---

[130] Assemblies of God, "Requirements," 2006. *Assemblies of God USA Web.* http://chaplaincy.ag.org/gen_requirements.cfm (7 Sept 2006).

# VOLUNTEER CHAPLAINS

During the Revolutionary War, clergy charged out the front doors of their churches right alongside their volunteer militia members to engage the enemy threatening their way of life. Volunteer chaplains are vital to chaplaincy ministry, often because there are not enough regular chaplains to fill the needs. In rural areas, it is hard to find chaplains for police and fire departments. Local ministers help the police and fire departments in their area by working as volunteer or part-time chaplains. If the needs are great, training, and experience requirements may be waived. In these cases, the chaplain starts working and gets trained on-the-job and by attending classes at night and on weekends, as necessary.

In just about every agency that employees chaplains, even if they have strict requirements for certification, it is possible to be a volunteer. If you are interested, inquire about their volunteer program and what the requirements are. Many agencies only require a few credentials and attendance at their volunteer training program, usually held on weeknights and weekends. In that case, you could work as a chaplain, gaining experience, while taking care of the requirements for full-time employment.

# CHAPTER 4 – LEADERSHIP DYNAMICS

Most of the literature about leadership focuses on the person leading the local church or parachurch organization. The traits for these leaders are often gleaned right out of the leadership studies of universities or the inspired writings of successful business people and pastors. Leaders are admonished and challenged to be all they can be to reach the zenith of their potential and possibilities. Leadership development books and programs emphasize personal character, leading skills, team building, personnel skills, and come with a heavy dose of scriptural references and personal anecdotes.

The results are often impressive when leadership students are able to put this advice into practice. Churches grow, congregations are blessed, the lost are saved, communities are changed, local and foreign missions are started and sustained, and it seems that God richly blesses all of these activities.

## CHAPLAINCY TOP LEADERSHIP

There are very few top leadership positions in chaplaincy. One type of chaplain leader might be the director or manager of a department, yet they will almost always be subordinate to someone: a business or agency CEO, Director, Coordinator, Chancellor, or General Manager. The exception to this case would be the chaplain who started their own business, or who rose to a higher position, like director of the agency, based on their experience and performance at the lower level, and their ability to function appropriately at the higher level. For example a Director of Pastoral Care for a hospice might aspire to be the Hospice Agency Director, if they had the training, experience, and background to earn the promotion.

The person called by God to be a chaplain often has a servanthood attitude. In that light, the aspiration for a higher leadership position might not be a viable goal–just seeking the position would be a disparity, but people do. Some people find themselves almost thrust into the top position for lack of other candidates.

One group of chaplains who might seek a leadership position are those called to the chaplaincy with a secular business and leadership background. These people might gravitate to a leadership position if the opportunity should arise. They might move to that position out of a desire to influence the people of the larger organization and be something of a spiritual rudder. If they lead other chaplains, perhaps as a Pastoral Care Director or Spiritual Care Coordinator, they could help to facilitate the training, morale, support, and logistics of that group, among other duties associated with the organization.

In the military, a chaplain is an officer and is a military leader by commission and position. The chaplain can rise higher in rank within the chaplaincy organization itself, but only with authority over other chaplains.

Then there are those people, most highly qualified to be chaplains, who have no business being corporate type leaders but choose that role for prestige or money or both, and thus wallow along doing the best they can while missing their real and full potential.

The chaplain in a top leadership position is more like the senior pastor of a church. There are many administrative, logistical, and parochial duties that must be attended to, including expected tasks like speaking, leading groups, and attending meetings. The top chaplain leader must be willing to exercise authority, direct actions, make decisions, coordinate activities and duties, and discipline others, as necessary.

In the church, associate pastors almost automatically gravitate to a senior position at the same church or another. But in something like hospital chaplaincy, there is a real sense that God has called the chaplain only to patient care. To move from being a chaplain to being the top person (i.e. Pastoral Care Director of the hospital) means giving up most or all patient care. To move to the higher position must be seriously considered and held in prayer, even if the chaplain has the talent and training for the position. On one hand the position could be seen as a worldly promotion, but as the same time it could be a heavenly demotion, where the chaplain is out of God's will for their life.

Leadership books are not particularly helpful in this area. They target non-leaders and current leaders who want to be better leaders or great leaders, and there is little middle ground. In other words, how do you lead without being the top person in the organization or a typical second chair person? The chaplain may find that it is more plausible to grow as a spiritual leader than to become the head of an organization.

If being a chaplain spiritual leader is also about passion, then Reggie McNeal said it right: "Great spiritual leaders can articulate their passion. They know what makes their heart beat faster. They know what they do that enables them to feel the smile of God. They move toward their passion. They feed it. They are intentioned and alive!"[131] I would suggest that if a chaplain feels this way about their ministry to people in need, they are great spiritual leaders to their patients, families, and staff. All of us in ministry want to be

---

[131] Reggie McNeal, *Practicing Greatness: 7 disciplines of extraordinary spiritual leaders* (San Francisco: Jossey-Bass, 2006), 88-9.

where God wants us and feel his smile upon us, so lead where you are planted until you are sure God is moving you to do something else.

## TRADITIONAL CHURCH LEADERSHIP

Everyone agrees that there are different types of leaders and that they have different types of ministries within the body of Christ–the church overall and in the local church: One body, many parts. The pastor is usually the head person with responsibility over the other parts. In 1 Corinthians 12, Paul uses the analogy of the body to show how the group of believers must work together and how each part is vital to the health of the other parts, and the body as a whole. He emphasizes that each part should have equal concern for the other parts. In his hierarchy, he mentions apostles and prophets, teachers and miracle workers, then healers, helps, administration, and speaking in tongues. The way Paul writes this, all of these positions have leadership qualities that work for the greater good, which is for the believers to reach maturity in Christ.

Again Paul writes,

It was he [Jesus] who gave some to be apostles, some to be prophets, some to be evangelists, and some to be pastors and teachers, to prepare God's people for works of service, so that the body of Christ may be built up until we all reach unity in the faith and in the knowledge of the Son of God and become mature, attaining the whole measure of the fullness of Christ.[132]

Local church ministry is not a one-person show and was never designed that way. By design, the local church is a collection of members who work together for the good of the body. That would mean that leadership, while working from top down, is distributed and authority is delegated. Leadership moves from top down because it starts with God,

---

[132] Eph 4:11-13.

and then goes to the person appointed as the leader of the group, who is held accountable to God and the people under them.

In the modern church, I'm not sure where all the apostles and prophets are located (I know some people claim to know). They might be those people with big, Godly visions and directions. Evangelists are easier to spot with people like Billy Graham on the national stage, and other evangelists leading revivals in the local church. Although some pastors and teachers reach national prominence, most of them bring foundation and stability at the local level.

Every tool that allows the pastors and teachers to do their job more effectively should be considered. To shepherd and teach, these leaders study to show themselves approved by others. "Do your best to present yourself to God as one approved, a workman who does not need to be ashamed and who correctly handles the word of truth."[133] This means that people under their leadership hold these leaders accountable and God holds them accountable. It is not a light thing to become a shepherd or teacher, because they are acting on God's behalf to bring nurture, love, and growth to his Church. Shepherding school often takes place on our knees at the foot of the bed, and the instructor is the Holy Spirit. Still, based on 2nd Timothy, pastors and teachers have an obligation to study everything that would make them better at their job: theology, counseling, and leadership, to name a few.

If the ministry is small, the pastor may do just about everything, including visiting the suffering and the needy. But if the ministry grows, people with more skills are able to step forward and minister. The person who visits the suffering is an important part of the body, although they may not have the title of chaplain.

---

[133] 2 Tim 2:15.

Another aspect of chaplain leadership that might be important is the focused approach that chaplaincy can bring to a church ministry. As professional, first-chair type leaders, chaplains are very focused on their ministry and role. Reggie Joiner wrote, "Experts tend to implement strategies that are much more effective, so churches that breed specialists have a clear advantage over churches that are full of generalists."[134] Chaplains that lead visitation ministries and train people to visit church members will bring a strength and depth to the program otherwise unimaginable. J. Oswald Sanders reminds us that, "God prepares leaders with a specific place and task in mind. Training methods are adapted to the mission, and natural and spiritual gifts are given with clear purpose."[135]

## PASTORAL AUTHORITY

Pastoral authority is the expectation people have in a church leader to exercise influence on them based on history, culture, and experience. The leader of a local Christian church is often called a pastor. That pastor has authority from either a denomination, organization, or congregation to carry out certain agreed upon teaching, rituals, and celebrations in a recognized and agreed upon format. So the pastor will marry, bury, baptize, teach, preach, and perform sacraments and rituals peculiar to the faith and beliefs of the people being led.

Chaplains are pastors of their organizations, wherever God has placed them. When a chaplain walks into a hospital room, whether the person believes in God or

---

[134] Reggie Joiner, Lane Jones, and Andy Stanley. *The 7 Practices of Effective Ministry*. (Sisters, OR: Multnomah, 2004), 113

[135] J. Oswald Sanders, *Spiritual Leadership: Principles of excellence for every believer*, (Chicago: Moody, 1994), 51.

believes something very different, they still walk in with a certain pastoral authority. The chaplain walks into the hospital room as a symbol, representing a *higher power*, whether the patient personally recognizes and respects that position or not. That authority is based on the same expectation people have of pastors. If the needy person has an expectation of authority and power, then the chaplain's ministry is well received, and elements like prayer and rituals become more powerful and efficacious.

In the hospital, a chaplain is hired and has pastoral authority based on the position held. But the acceptance and the success of the chaplain/patient interaction is based on the patient's history, previous experience, and expectation based on their faith, religion, and exposure to other ministers. The patient with a previously positive experience anticipates another. And the patient can see the chaplain as an extension of their own church ministry, which usually guarantees a favorable ministry outcome.

One of the patients at our hospice did not want to see a chaplain. Although raised a Lutheran, as an adult he had lived his own life, on his own terms, and did not have anything to do with God or church. Several months passed and his health began to fail quickly. One day he asked his wife to call and have the chaplain come by. The next day I followed his wife into the bedroom, and she announced, "Honey, the chaplain is here." He cried out, "Oh good, I need to get right with God!" What followed was a time of healing and reconciliation. He died the next morning and this verse came to my mind, "Is not this man a burning stick snatched from the fire?"[136]

There was a sense that I was the right person in the right place to minister to someone who otherwise might not have been ministered to. This person was far outside the church but of concern to God. Often chaplaincy seems to work on the fringes of

---

[136] Zech 3:2b.

95

society and the traditional church picking up the lost, the hurt, the suffering, and the damaged. At times, chaplaincy reminds me of the Good Samaritan story, because so many people have been damaged by church with the myriad feelings surrounding hurts, pride, and misunderstanding. Sometimes the chaplain is the only other person coming down that road as someone lays battered and bleeding in the ditch of life.

The daughter of one of the hospice patients asked me to come by, and when I arrived, her mother went in the bedroom, closed the door, and refused to see me. I asked the daughter to let her know that I did not come to judge her, but to just be a friend. The daughter called a week later and asked me to come out, as her mother was more receptive and closer to dying. I went out and learned that she had not been in the Catholic church since her divorce many years before, when a priest told her she was no longer welcome. I knelt by her bed, took her hands, and asked her to forgive me for the wrongs done to her. She wept. We prayed, asked for forgiveness, peace of mind, and the comfort of the Holy Spirit. She died two days later.

## INFLUENCE

One definition of a leader is someone who influences another.[137] It is impossible to state factually that influence simply equals leadership. The moon influences the earth, but the leader in that realm is actually the sun. If one person influences another, we might suggest that they have been in some kind of contact. Again, that is not necessarily influence. If I passed you on the street, tipped my hat and gave you a big smile and enthusiastically said, "Good morning!" I might positively influence the rest of your day without being a true leader in your life.

---

[137] Maxwell, *Developing the Leader*, 1.

Influence implies that one person, a leader, has an impact on another. The impacted person may or may not be compelled to follow or even react in a particular way, and the influence may not be obvious, or it may become insignificant. Sometimes the leadership influence is powerful and at other times it is subtle, yet it takes place. Simply put, it is interrelational–takes two people.

If a person said, "That person impressed me," we could say they were influenced: action and reaction. One person's action causes a response, reaction in another. In our daily lives, as we relate to the people around us, we cause influence, and we experience the influence of others. It seems that influence going out from one person to another requires a response. Philosophically and theologically, light requires eyes to enjoy it; it is mandatory. So influence that is helpful, gracious, loving, blessed, healing, nurturing, and reviving is often warmly received by another person.

But an influential person is not necessarily a leader. I propose the following definition of leadership and influence: *For influence to be leadership, the influence exerted by one person must engender a change response in the other's life.* The leadership must make a difference. The influential person, the leader, however subtly, for better or worse, changes a life.

With this definition chaplains are leaders, as they meet people in their darkest valleys and deepest needs. The chaplain influences people who are desperate for influence from a spiritual source, and very often lives are changed.

In that sense, it might be argued that the influence is more powerful because of anticipation. Because of preconceived ideas and experience with pastoral authority, clergy, or other chaplains, the person is more open to ministry and has an idea of what to expect. The person expects a positive influential experience, and if the chaplain delivers that, then they are satisfied with the ministry.

## First Chair Influence

By definition, first chair people are able to lead based on influence. Influence can grow and become more powerful, based on the words and actions of the leader. What sustains and grows the leadership influence is the person's personality, character, and presence, how they speak, how they treat people, and their reputation. As they grow personally, as their reputation grows, the influence grows, and their impact on people and ministries grows. When the leader treats everyone with respect, grow in their leadership and ministry abilities, and grow spiritually, their influence, reputation, and effectiveness grow.

The leader must be open to the idea of continued growth in all of these areas to maintain the leadership influence at a high level that meets the needs of an ever changing group of people. But the foundation created earlier in the ministry can sustain the leader long after the reasons for the original influence have faded away.

When a congregation interviews potential first chair leaders, something about what they say and their presence and personality influences the committee to make a favorable decision about their employment. People hire leaders and potential leaders based on that influence, reputation, and expectations developed from the interview.

Devote and faithful followers support the leader based on their shared history, but the ministry will show marked declines over time in different areas as new people come who do not share the original basis of the influence. Senior pastors, who feel that their influence has waned, should be grooming their successor and helping them grow in influence and responsibility.

## SECOND CHAIR INFLUENCE

Second chair leadership is about the influence the assistant has in a subordinate position within the organization. The influence developed by the second chair person determines their ability to lead, the quality of their leadership, and their effectiveness. If they do not have influence, they probably do not have a leadership effect in that position.

Second chair influence can be nurtured and grow, but it is also contingent on the leadership maturity of the first chair leader. If the first chair leader feels threatened by the second chair person, the second chair person's influence will always be marginalized. Likewise, if the first chair person has the emotional maturity to mentor the second chair leader and help them develop and nurture influence and leadership traits, the overall ministry will flourish and the second chair leader will grow as a first chair leader.

## SECOND CHAIR LEADERSHIP

The first chair leader is the top person of a church or organization. The second chair leader works for, with, and supports the first chair person. *Second chairs*, as they are called, are the number two people: executive pastors, associates, administrators, and leaders of ministries within the larger organization. These people often lead and influence others and are themselves subordinate to the first chair person.

Authority is delegated from the first chair person to the second chair person or people, and on down. In that light, the second chair person might have more or less authority depending on the personality, ego, and maturity of the first chair person, their leadership style, and the actual or perceived needs of the organization. Leadership literature teaches that the delegation of authority is important to team building and ministry growth. Assuming positive intent, people in ministry want to do a good job and must be equipped with the tools, hence the authority, to perform that job and to be successful.

Second chair leaders try to build influence in the church to be more effective leaders and better support the first chair person. "The habit of looking across the broader organization is a distinguishing trait of second chair leaders. They may not be involved in every decision or every ministry, but their perspective is organization wide. They are able to add value throughout."[138] Their effectiveness is contingent on many factors, some they control and some they don't. How well they enjoy this season of ministry is largely dependent on their attitude, the people in the church, and the working dynamics of the people they work for and with.

Chaplains are second chair leaders in one sense, because they support leaders above them in almost every organization they serve. But their authority does not come from someone above them; it is not delegated down, like it is for second chair leaders. Chaplains derive their authority directly from God. It is pastoral authority.


SPIRITUAL LEADERSHIP

If leadership is about influence, then spiritual leadership is about influence on the spiritual level. Some areas of spiritual influence are issues of transcendence, connections, meaning, contentment, relationships, support, grief, loss, hope, coping, values, ethics,

---

[138] Mike Bonem and Roger Patterson, *Leading from the Second Chair: Serving your church, fulfilling your role, and realizing your dreams* (San Francisco: Jossey-Bass, 2005), 16.

sacred tradition, sacraments, music, ritual, presence, beliefs, prayer, meditation, reconciliation, and end of life. Spiritual leadership can touch the heart of people where they feel most needy and vulnerable, and the impact is often powerful and long lasting. And in some cases, this leadership impact can be a matter of life and death.

In *The Wounded Healer*, the chapter on *Principles of Christian Leadership*, Nouwen writes that Christian leadership is:

> First, personal concern, which asks one man to give his life for his fellow man; second, a deep-rooted faith in the value and meaning of life, even when the days look dark; and third, an outgoing hope which always looks for tomorrow, even beyond the moment of death. And all these principles are based on the one and only conviction that, since God has become man, it is man who has the power to lead his fellow man to freedom.[139]

The leader with personal concern, deep-rooted faith, and outgoing hope has to really care about people, love God intimately, and hope strongly and against all odds. This speaks closely to the ministry of chaplains.

Leaders with this focus are not well suited for the pace and demands of leadership in a church striving for growth and outreach. They may attend the striving church for a variety of reasons, but then work in something like the visitation ministry, or they may attend that church and serve elsewhere, like the chaplaincy in a hospital. This is the case for me. I attend a local church that is a vital and growing ministry and has many outreaches to the community and overseas. I help out occasionally in a variety of areas, but I am not in a staff or ministry leadership position.

---

[139] Henri J.M. Nouwen, *The Wounded Healer* (New York: Doubleday, 1972), 71.

WOMEN IN CHAPLAINCY

Over the ages, when men have gone to war, women have been nearby, if not in the thick

of battle. Some women, like Joan of Arc are well known, and Celtic women were

renowned warriors and led men into battle.

> The Roman historian Plutarch described a battle in 102 B.C. between Romans and
> Celts: "The fight had been no less fierce with the women than with the men
> themselves . . . the women charged with swords and axes and fell upon their
> opponents uttering a hideous outcry."[140]

For thousands of years, women followed armies tending to their husbands,

treating the sick and wounded, and helping with supply and cooking needs. Women have

volunteered in every war to support their loved ones and the military cause. Likewise,

women held families together at home while their men went off to war. So it's not

surprising to find women going off to war in the United States and serving as chaplains

whenever possible.

During the Civil War, the 1st Wisconsin Regiment of Heavy Artillery asked Mrs.

Ella Hobart to be their chaplain. Mrs. Hobart was a minister with the Religion-

Philosophical Society in Illinois but was not ordained by them. The unit was stationed at

Fort Stevens and possibly saw combat while she was there (Ft Stevens was built to

defend the northern routes into Washington D.C.). Someone, probably her commander,

sent a letter to President Lincoln asking that she be commissioned. Lincoln wrote

Secretary of War, Edwin M. Stanton saying that he did not oppose the commission, but

would leave the decision to commission her up to him. Secretary Stanton denied her

---

[140] Lothene Experimental Archeology, "Women as Warriors-Celtic and Roman," *Lothene Web*.
http://www.lothene.demon.co.uk/others/womenrom.html (28 Oct 2006).

commission based on the fact that she was a woman and not ordained. After serving nine

months with the unit, she went home.[141]

As the number of women grew in the military, the need for female chaplains

grew. A hundred and ten years after the Civil War, the first female chaplain received her

commission in the United States Army. On July 8, 1974, the Reverend Alice M.

Henderson of the African Methodist Episcopal Church became a 2nd Lieutenant and the

first black female chaplain.

In 1995, Chaplain Carol A. Van Schenkhof wrote,

> I suppose I have been lucky. None of my commanders have opposed having a
> female chaplain. I believe female chaplains serve as positive role models for
> female soldiers. Many times female soldiers come and confide in me. They have
> said they were glad to have a female chaplain to relate to. Since I was a "Family
> Member" for ten years, I can relate to family members very well. I understand
> their situations and feelings since I was in their shoes.[142]

In 1984, Rabbi Bonnie Koppell became the first Jewish female chaplain in the

military and served in the Army Reserves. Rabbi Koppell wrote the following about

being a female chaplain:

> Chaplains are noncombatants—we do not carry weapons, we are not trained to
> fight. We are there to minister to the religious needs of the troops and, as such, we
> are an essential part of the military force. No one likes war, no one wants war. No
> one prays for peace with more fervor than the soldier who stands ready to lay
> down his or her life for our country. Yet, I am not a pacifist; I believe that there
> are times when war is justified. War is always a horrible tragedy, but it is not
> necessarily immoral. I am proud to consider among my many identities as wife, as
> mother, as rabbi, as teacher, as friend, yet another—as an American soldier. God
> forbid the need should arise, our Jewish soldiers deserve to have rabbis who are
> trained and ready to deploy alongside them, to be there to offer all the support
> they will need. I am proud to be among those who stand ready to go with them.[143]

---

[141] Norton, *Struggling for Recognition*, 2:86.
[142] Brinsfield, *Encouraging Faith*, 6:340.
[143] Jewish Women's Archive, "Koppell." *Jewish Women's Archive Web.*
http://www.jwa.org/discover/inthepast/infocus/military/chaplains/koppell.html (19 Oct 2006).

In response to Desert Storm in 1991, Army Reservist Rabbi Chana Timoner was transferred to the active Army and became the first active duty female Rabbi chaplain. She served on the hospital staff at Fort Sam Houston, San Antonio, Texas, where they treated the sick and wounded veterans coming home from the Middle East.

On July 22, 2004, the first Buddhist chaplain was commissioned in the military, who was also a woman. In 1988, Gracie Shin joined the Marines and served four years. After she completed that tour of duty, she earned her B.A. in religion and philosophy at George Mason University, Fairfax, Virginia, and attended seminary at the Graduate Theological Union/Institute of Buddhist Studies in Berkeley, California. In a ceremony at the Pentagon, in an area repaired after the destruction of September 11th, Lt (Junior Grade) Gracie Shin was sworn in as a Navy Reserve Chaplain and began serving at the Naval Reserve Center in Alameda, California.[144]

Female chaplains have served in hospitals for a long time, although not necessarily with the official title of chaplain. Different Catholic orders have built hospitals over the years.

In 1855, Mrs. Anna Marie Boll Bachmann (widow), her sister, Barbara Boll, and a friend, Anna Dorn with permission from Pope Pius IX started the order, the Sisters of Francis of Philadelphia. At their investment, their names were changed: Anna Maria Boll Bachmann became Sister Mary Francis, Barbara Boll became Sister Margaret, and Anna Dorn became Sister Bernardine. They soon attracted other followers. The sisters tended the poor and sick in their convents or the homes of the patients, fed all who came to their doors, hosted immigrant women, and taught school.

---

[144] Navy News. "First Armed Forces Buddhist Chaplain Commissioned." 22 Jul 2004. *Navy News Web.* http://www.news.navy.mil/search/display.asp?story_id=14387 (17 Oct 2006).

In 1858, there was a serious smallpox epidemic, and the sisters helped all of the people they could. But Mother Mary Francis didn't think it was enough, so she made plans to open her own hospital. She wrote:

> There is not a hospital in the entire city of Philadelphia where they accept patients with contagious diseases or poor people. We are convinced that God helps us and blesses our work; we have numerous proofs of that. We feed so many poor who come to the door. . . . As long as God does not stop giving to us, we shall not stop giving to the poor.[145]

In 1860, Mother Mary Francis of the Sisters of Francis of Philadelphia started St Mary's Hospital of Philadelphia. St. Joseph Medical Center in Tacoma, Washington was started in 1899 by the Sisters of Francis of Philadelphia. St. Joseph Medical Center is part of the larger Franciscan Health System and Catholic Health Initiatives.

Today, Franciscan Health System and the community of hospitals and clinics it represents, still hold to the core values of the founding sisters. As a faith-based organization, they understand and the importance of spiritual care in conjunction with physical care–caring for the whole person. The work of chaplains and the Catholic sisters in their hospitals is highly valued, and they are seen by all staff (doctors, nurses, and administrators) as integral members of the patient healing team.

FEMALE CHAPLAIN LEADERSHIP

Unlike the church, there are many more opportunities for female clergy and lay in the chaplaincy, because the chaplaincy is about inclusiveness and meeting the particular needs of a group of people. Hospitals and hospices, in particular, hire many female chaplains.

---

[145] Order of the Sisters of St. Francis of Philadelphia, "History," *Sisters of St Francis of Philadelphia Web.* http://www.osfphila.org/sp/about_us/history.html (21 Oct 2006).

In Catholic hospitals in the past (more than twenty-five years ago), Catholic Sisters often transitioned from nursing to pastoral care as they got closer to retirement.[146] They were often seen more as *pastoral associates*, assisting the priests in their ministrations, rather than full chaplains. Although this is an older account, it speaks to the sentiment of the time: "A Sister who is an interdenominational chaplain in a large public hospital, and also a supervisor in the CPE training program, spoke disparagingly of some priests who 'come in at nine-thirty and go home at three and think they have done a day's work. They have no concept of professional pastoral care.' "[147]

I have worked with female chaplains at St. Joseph Medical Center in Tacoma, Washington. Some are sisters of the Sisters of Francis of Philadelphia order, and others are lay people from different backgrounds, including nursing and teaching, who felt called to minister to the sick. They are all readily accepted by staff, patients, and fellow chaplains, and their ministry is very effective, wherever they work in the hospital.

Women chaplaincy is more predictable than parish ministry. The hours are scheduled, whereas in the parish, you can get called at almost any time. People in the parish have certain expectations, and one is that their pastor be available at all times to help them in a crisis. With the diversity of people and their reasonable and unreasonable expectations, parish ministry can be brutal at times.[148]

In the hospital, the chaplain goes to the place of crisis and need, ministers as necessary, then goes home. They may see the patient many times or just once depending on their particular situation. People in the hospital are more accepting and open to female

---

[146] Joseph H. Fichter, *Religion and Pain: The spiritual dimensions of health care* (New York: Crossroad, 1981), 111-3.
[147] Fichter, *Religion and Pain*, 112.
[148] Krusemark, Interview 14 Nov 2006.

ministry, because their needs, fears, and suffering trumps their prejudices. Also, the hospital often feels like neutral territory when it comes to gender biases and discrimination, because women are predominant as nurses, doctors, social workers, and of course, chaplains.

New female chaplains sometimes need to claim the authority that is intrinsic to the clergy position. Most hospital patients are open to female chaplains, or they might take a wait-and-see attitude if they come from a religious tradition without female clergy. So if the female chaplain acts like the minister she is, the ministry will almost always be effective and fruitful, and people will respond positively. Another way of stating it would be, *You are in a leadership position, be the chaplain.*

Claiming the authority and being the chaplain has a lot to do with training. Without the training, the chaplain has to find her way around and figure out what it is that she does and how she does it. With training (i.e. CPE and/or seminary), issues of identity, authenticity, and the exercise of pastoral authority come out and are developed and nurtured. Dr. Robert Clinton talked about leadership and the developmental training processes when he wrote:

> As a leader, you should recognize that God is continually developing you over a lifetime. His top priority is to conform you to the image of Christ for ministry with spiritual authority. Enduring fruitfulness flows out of being. In addition, to transforming your character, God will increase your capacity to influence through developing spiritual gifts.[149]

---

[149] J. Robert Clinton, *The Making of a Leader: Recognizing the lessons and stages of leadership development*, (Colorado Springs: NavPress, 1988), 54.

# SERVANTHOOD

"Whoever wants to become great among you must be your servant, and whoever wants to be the first must be the slave of all."[150] This verse is often promoted as a mantra for leadership aspirations, but it speaks about rejecting the self and the promotion of others. It is about servanthood. Can a true servant of others be a leader? Can a 21st century Christian be a powerful leader in the kingdom of God by simply serving others at the expense of their own ego? The Mark 10:43-44 definition of leadership more exactly fits the ministry of chaplaincy. A true servant can be a leader, but it is a byproduct of the action, not the goal. Jesus washed feet and sought to serve others at all times. Yet, he was a dynamic leader. His servant influence, working in the power of the Holy Spirit, was powerful and touched people deeply.

If Jesus was here today, he might visit a megachurch, but I'm not sure he would to want to lead that church, as he would find it too restricting for his leadership style. If this had been his style, he probably would have set up shop permanently in the Great Temple in Jerusalem. Instead, he became an itinerant preacher, outside on the edges of the church, traveling around the countryside with his followers, creating church wherever he stopped. That place might be a person's home, mountainsides, hilltops, vineyards, the courtyard of the synagogue, or olive gardens. In this respect, the chaplaincy ministry is very similar.

"You know that those who are regarded as rulers of the Gentiles lord it over them, and their high officials exercise authority over them. Not so with you."[151] Jesus is comparing worldly/secular leadership with believer/Christian leadership. In this context,

---

[150] Mark 10:43b-44a.
[151] Matt 20:25.

he states that greatness and firstness come from sacrificial actions. The influence of the person who acts out of the interests of others makes them great and makes them first. I'm not sure the position of greatness or firstness Jesus is referring to is always enjoyed in this world. It is often the reward received in heaven for a life well-lived in God's service. "His master replied, 'Well done, good and faithful servant! You have been faithful with a few things; I will put you in charge of many things. Come and share your master's happiness!' "[152]

God is always looking for quality over quantity. What does God require, and how would he explain servanthood? "He has showed you, O man, what is good. And what does the Lord require of you? To act justly and to love mercy and to walk humbly with you God."[153] Broken down it reads: *Walk with God and be just, merciful, and humble.* "The sacrifices of God are a broken spirit; a broken and contrite heart, O God, you will not despise."[154]

> Leaders who fix their gaze on the horizon, hoping for something better rather than focusing on the tasks at hand, are unworthy to hold their current positions. Conversely, leaders who enthusiastically invest their energies into each new assignment God grants them will enjoy success where they are, but they will also develop the character God looks for to use for further, expanded service…People often look for tangible results such as head counts or profit margins, but these only serve as partial indicators of what God considers success. The accomplishment of God's purposes is the only complete and infallible indication of success.[155]

The person in ministry with a keen leadership drive and a certain business acumen will gravitate to the ministry that has potential to grow, and where they can make a difference. Paul had a global vision and ministry, and that is what God expected of him.

---

[152] Matt 25:21.
[153] Mic 6:8.
[154] Psalm 51:17.
[155] Henry T. Blackaby, and Richard Blackaby, *Spiritual Leadership: Moving people on to God's agenda,* (Nashville: Broadman & Holman, 2001), 110-1.

His reward will be based on what God had for him, and how he responded to that call. He was given a certain number of talents and invested them.

In the Parable of the Talents, Jesus explains that one man received five talents, the second man received two talents, and the third received one talent.[156] When the master returned, he inquired as to how they had used the talents entrusted to them. He rewarded those who had used their talents wisely and could show gains for what they were given. I believe it is the same for leaders. We are responsible for the talents, literally, and abilities that God gives us in order to show gain. He gives us talents and abilities and gifts of the Spirit to edify and build up the church. God invests in us. We invest in others. We respond by using these talents, abilities and gifts to serve others and thus gender a return on what he gave us. If God calls someone to a mega ministry, they must be faithful in completing their task. If God calls someone to minister to the dying, they must be faithful to their task. That does not mean that one person is less of a leader than the other; the more important hope is that both are faithful with the talents God gave them. Leaders called by God to ministry, whether they serve in the church, on its edges, or outside the walls will be wildly successful in God's eyes, whatever the numbers and the size, if they walk with him in justice, mercy and humility.

When is service more important than ambition? Perhaps it is better phrased as this question: Is foot washing a leadership trait? Jesus said, "I am among you as one who serves."[157] Would anyone doubt Jesus' leadership abilities? Yet, we promote the Gentile version of leadership as the preferred and biblical model for those people seeking to lead believers. It is important to find balance.

---

[156] Matt 25:14-30.
[157] Luke 22:27.

The church as we know it today has evolved from the time of Jesus. We are taught that if leadership is excellent, the church that meets in a building will grow and thrive and have much impact on the community and world around them.[158] When many pastors put leadership training into effect, they often benefit from that effort. Is bigger better? Is it God's perfect will or is it God's permissiveness allowing people to launch *best practices,* Harvard business school style endeavors with the hopes of God's blessing? It certainly seems like God is blessing, because so many people are saved, the lost are reached, and the ministry if flourishing. The results are impressive. But is that what God wants church leaders to be doing?

I would propose that if a leader is doing God's will and fulfilling the purpose God gave them, and they are doing it with the best of their ability in the Lord, then greatness is a byproduct that is not sought for its own sake. The pastor of a humble church in a struggling poor neighborhood, who is doing God's will and is where God placed them, has just as great a reward in heaven as the person called to lead millions to the Lord in a mega church and world-wide endeavor. Wherever leaders are called, they want to be able to simply say, "I have done my best with what you gave me."

---

[158] Bill Hybels, *Courageous Leadership* (Grand Rapids: Zondervan, 2002), 69.

# CHAPTER 5 – THE CHAPLAIN LEADER MANAGER

Sometimes chaplains move into leadership and management positions and either fail or perform marginally. This happens because the chaplain's success as a leader in their ministry is not a good indication of how well they will perform as managers. I've seen people with wonderful chaplain-patient skills, who had poor people skills and team member skills when it came to working with their peers. Likewise, the skills required for leadership and management are different, although closely related. Having one skill does not guarantee success with the other.

A chaplain has different skills than a church leader. Leadership skills for working in the hospital as a chaplain are not the same as the leadership skills required for running a church, directing the pastoral care office, or building a business around an idea for a chaplaincy ministry.

Clergy leadership is based on pastoral authority, influence, and the congregation's expectations. The senior pastor of a church has leadership and management skills similar to a business person, because it involves working with people to reach goals. Since chaplains rarely run anything, like a business or a church, this leadership skill set is often foreign to them.

Typically, the leader sets the direction and focus for the manager, who supervises people focused on accomplishing tasks and reaching goals. The manager's leadership and influence are limited to their group of people. This is also the difference between first chair and second chair leaders.

Although leaders and managers have distinct roles, traits, and skills that compliment each other, they often overlap. Sometimes leading and managing differences are listed in such a way as to make the leader look celestial and the manager look like an oaf. I reject this because it promotes one set of leadership skills at the expense of the other. Instead, they actually compliment each other, and a person can find themselves performing both skill sets simultaneously. In other words, there are leaders and managers, and there are leader managers. And there are managers who are about to become leaders, who exhibit both skill sets.

"To know how to do a job is the accomplishment of labor; to be available to tell others is the accomplishment of the teacher; to inspire others to do better work is the accomplishment of management; to be able to do all three is the accomplishment of true leaders."[159] In this passage, John Maxwell distinguishes between the various roles people play in accomplishing a task. This principle tells us that in certain situations, the skills for each area (worker, teacher, manager, leader) can overlap. A person can be the sole leader of an organization requiring them to wear many hats: lead, manage, teach, and do the work necessary for success. Leader managers are those people using a blend of skills sets to accomplish their goal.

Leading means you are out in front and pointing the way. The leader is saying *go here, do this, try this, look over there,* while the manager works to make it happen. When the manager and leader are the same person, then the skills blend into the following five traits:

---

[159] Maxwell, *Developing the Leader*, 113.

Leader managers are long-term thinkers who see beyond the day's crisis and the quarterly report. Leader managers' interests in their companies do not stop with the units they head. They want to know how all the company's departments affect one another, and they are constantly reaching beyond their specific areas of influence. Leader managers put heavy emphasis on vision, values, and motivation. Leader managers have strong political skills to cope with conflicting requirements of multiple constituents. Leader managers don't accept the status quo. [160]

Management has been described as an art and science, where good skills in decision-making, planning, organizing, and supervising are most important. Skills can be learned, and training and experience improve a person's ability to manage. There are many books on leadership and management. Some promote tried-and-true techniques and skills, some come up with a new twist on an old idea, and occasionally there is something new. In *Smart Moves for People in Charge*, the authors list one hundred and thirty checklists for helping a person become a better leader and manager, and each checklist covers a myriad of things: *Twelve Ways to Improve Your Listening, Fourteen Rules for Chairing a Meeting, Sixteen Phrases of Great Leadership*, and one hundred and twenty-seven more. [161] The book is great and I have many pages tabbed for easy reference, but by itself these lists will not make you a manager or a leader.

Over the last thirty years, I have owned my own business, and have worked in administration, training, management, operations, and logistics. In each career path, I received lot of leadership and management training and have been very successful. I have attended leadership and management schools, seminars, trained supervisors and managers, and have read many books on these subjects. Now I want to synthesize all of this down into three basic principles that can serve as a starting point particularly for the chaplain leader manager.

---

[160] Maxwell, *Developing the Leader*, iv.
[161] Sam Deep and Lyle Sussman, *Smart Moves for People in Charge* (New York: Addison-Wesley, 1995), 72, 88, 98.

One thing I learned early on is the premier importance of treating people with respect. I can't emphasize enough how important this is in being a successful leader and manager. Everything else falls under this principle. How you treat people is a reflection of your character and maturity. Treating people with respect, whether above you or below you in the organization's structure, causes you to grow in influence. If you respect and encourage your people, value their contributions, show them you are committed to their well-being and success, and promote integrity and character in them and yourself, you will always be successful.

> In biblical times and in modern corporations, people have enthusiastically followed leaders who cared about them. "They don't care how much you know until they know how much you care" is not an empty cliché. Again and again, it has been shown that true caring creates more employee loyalty and (ironically) better "hard" results than cold exhortations to do more and produce more.[162]

Second, you must know yourself: what motivates you, your leadership and management styles, how you handle change, criticism, a crisis, stress, personnel problems, demands on your time from below and above, how you solve problems, and a host of other things. If you do not know yourself, you will probably never really know your people. People are complicated and messy, so if you do not handle change, criticism, and stress well, you will not manage yourself or your people well. Do a self-appraisal and ask yourself if you have the qualifications, personally and through experience, to move into a higher position of responsibility in leadership and management.

The third most important concept is to become the expert in your field. If you want to become the Pastoral Care Director at the medical center, you must know that

---

[162] Lorin Woolfe, *Leadership Secrets from the Bible: From Moses to Matthew-Management Lessons for Contemporary Leaders*, (New York: MJF Books, 2002), 64.

hospital inside and out, what makes the organization work, their business strategy, what the priorities are, and your role in the grand scheme of things. It might mean you need training and experience in hospital administration, which is often required before getting the position. On occasion, the training and experience could be learned afterwards on the job, if the people hiring you are comfortable with that, and believe it is possible for these things to be learned based on demonstrated experience and skills in other areas. Continued education ensures that you will become and stay the expert, and a willingness to keep learning will greatly benefit you, your employees, and the organization.

How do you measure success? If you do not really qualify for the management position, getting it could increase your income and pride, but hurt your soul and the people you work for and with. The upside to getting a management position is the actual or perceived increase in money, power, and prestige. If that is the only reason you want to be a leader or manager, then your ambition and motivation are unbiblical, and I can say with conviction that you are out of God's will for your life, and you have pride issues.

The power a manager receives is based on how well the employees perform. A manager has authority, the way a chaplain has pastoral authority. The manager is granted authority to run the department by those over them, but if the people do not respect the manager or respond positively to this authority, then the manager is effectively powerless and will soon be out of a job.

President Harry S. Truman had a sign on his desk that read, *The BUCK STOPS here!* , in reference to the old expression of *passing the buck.*[163] As a leader manager, you have the position and all that comes with it, which also includes responsibility for legal

---

[163] Truman Presidential Museum and Library, "The Buck Stop," *Truman Library Web.* http://www.trumanlibrary.org/buckstop.htm (9 Nov 2006).

and financial issues, and the actions of your employees. If a hospital chaplain moves into management, it often means leaving patient care behind.

The chaplain is responsible only for their ministry and the skills they bring to patient care, and they get almost immediate feedback from people they minister to on how well they do their job. But as the manager, you seldom get immediate feedback, and may not get any, in some areas, for a year. For example, how well you do on the annual budget, managing your financials and labor, impacts your end-of-year evaluations. Also, you can be held legally liable if you do not respond appropriately to a sexual harassment charge, and then be fired because you did handled it right, but did it too late.

If you are thinking about a management position, listen to your heart, take it to God in prayer, and speak with people you respect and who know you. Then you have to be honest about what God tells you, and what your friends tell you. There are six possibilities. You might be told *never, no, yes, maybe, yes but wait,* or *get some training and reevaluate this move later. Never* you can understand, although you might not want to hear the reasons. If the answer is *no,* that might not mean *never,* and that something may be possible in the future. Ask God and them why they said *no,* or *wait,* or *maybe.* Perhaps there is an area of your life that needs work. It might depend on if you are able and willing to do this work, or if it is even possible. Show some respect for God and them and yourself by following their direction.

If you get approval from God and peers to move into a leadership and/or management position in an organization, this scripture applies to you. "The Lord has sought out a person after the Lord's own heart and appointed them a leader of the people."[164] Do your work as unto the Lord and enjoy this new phase of ministry.

---

[164] 1 Sam 13:14 (my interpretation without gender).

# CHAPTER 6 – CHAPLAIN MINISTRY DYNAMICS

In this section, I want to discuss the idea of first chair leadership and determine where chaplains fit into that dynamic. Then I want to look at where chaplains come from and how they lead in their ministry. The section on the theology of pastoral care and the section on ethics in chaplain leadership help us take a closer look at the inner workings of the ministry and leadership issues.

Most people's lives take place outside the walls of the traditional church. Not being *church-goers,* means they are unavailable to the local minister and ministry. And being outside the church means that when the crises of life descend upon them, they are not readily able to access the spiritual leadership they need at a crucial moment in their lives.

Chaplains are able to bring the ministry of the church to people when and where they are most needy, most vulnerable, and suffering. In this respect, chaplains are pastors without walls, and are an essential part of the body of Christ, and its evangelical and ministerial effect on the world.

One advantage chaplains have in this area of ministry is that they are not concerned about the administration of a local church, church politics, and in many cases, how they will get paid. Freedom from these issues means that chaplains do not have any other church agenda on their minds when visiting the needy than to be fully present and helpful.

Chaplains take the lead when circumstances warrant it, but they are not often considered leaders in their own right. When a justice issue or an ethical dilemma present themselves, it is not uncommon for the chaplain to champion the cause. Given the circumstances, the chaplain may just offer advice, counsel, and guidance, or they may fight tooth and nail for what they believe is right, for the good of the person or people they represent.

## FIRST CHAIR DYNAMICS

By definition, first chair leaders want to fix things and make things happen. Bill Hybels, leader of Willow Creek Community Church of South Barrington, Illinois, says he is on the lunatic fringe when it comes to his emotional state.[165] There is a sense of constant striving, pushing, pulling, and anxiety.

Chaplains are more concerned with meeting people where they are at. The chaplain is not opposed to fixing and healing, but it is not necessarily the end result they are looking for. The chaplain understands that God is at work in the patient *and in the chaplain.* It is more important to show up and be fully present.

I have seen first chair pastors in the hospital visiting patients, but I have seen many more second chair ministers visiting their members. I wonder if it is because sick people can't readily be *fixed*, and their continued decline and death is seen as a failure? Or, is it just an economy of time issue, and first chair leaders decide where best to spend their precious time?

The first chair person has to decide what is important and why. If they decide that the hospital is not the best use of their talents and time, then it is important that they

---

[165] Hybels, *Courageous Leadership*, 64.

120

organize people to fill that void. In many churches, the hospital ministry and visitation ministry are passed off to those people who feel called to be with the sick and dying, and the aged.

## A THEOLOGY OF PASTORAL CARE

Theology of pastoral care is important in understanding what motivates chaplains, and how they understand their calling. There can be as many theologies of pastoral care as there are chaplains. It is important that chaplains take the time to think this through and develop their own.

One theology of pastoral care in chaplaincy is based on my understanding of the ministry of presence and incarnation. Presence and incarnation means being a representative of Christ: being his hands, his voice, his presence, available and wholly present, to people in need. In my own case, my ministry of presence and incarnation developed through my struggles with arthritis in my neck, back, and feet. When the pain is intense and prolonged, I spend more time in prayer and meditation and have come to depend on God for the comfort that only he can give. "Praise be to the God and Father of our Lord Jesus Christ, the Father of all compassion and the God of all comfort, who comforts us in all our troubles, so that we can comfort those in any trouble with the comfort we ourselves have received from God."[166] I would suggest that my struggles with pain have allowed me to be a compassionate incarnational presence to those I minister to.

Bonhoeffer in *Life Together* wrote, "The ministry of listening has been committed to [chaplains] by him who is himself the Great Listener, and whose work we could share.

---

[166] 2 Cor 1:3-4.

We should listen with the ears of God that we may speak the Word of God."[167] (brackets mine) Many of my patients who are coming to the end of their lives (I have ministered in Oncology, Renal Dialysis and Hospice) want, more than anything, to be heard–to tell their story. They want to be heard not as patients, but as human souls. It seems that people seldom find someone who will just listen to their story and not want to tell their own. I seek to listen attentively to what they have to say: listening respectfully, non-judgmentally, and compassionately; and in hearing their story, come alongside them with empathy in their time of need and/or change. How does this help manifest itself? Sometimes just by being there, listening, and holding their hand: a ministry of presence.

The hospice staff could not figure out why Don was still hanging on. As I listened to Don tell his stories, one theme kept popping out: he and his step-mom did not get along at all. She suffered from mental illness at a time when it was common to keep it a family secret, and she made him suffer terribly. In time we talked about his relationship with his mom, who had died years before. We talked about reconciliation and forgiveness. He understood that the mental illness probably played a huge role in how she treated him, herself, and others. He died peacefully not long after working this out.

Another idea in this theology of pastoral care in chaplaincy is what I call the incarnation of the circular Jesus in suffering. "The Lord is close to the brokenhearted and saves those who are crushed in spirit."[168] Life brings loss and grief and occasional crises. As chaplains we are often close to the brokenhearted and those crushed in spirit; in pain, disappointment, depression, misery, despair, fear, sorrowful, groaning, anguish, and

---

[167] Dietrich Bonhoeffer, *Life Together* (New York: HarperCollins, 1954), 54.
[168] Psalm 34:18.

burdened. Sometimes we are the first people to meet with them and their families as they encounter painful situations and ponder heartbreaking news.

> Jesus said, "For I was hungry and you gave me something to eat, I was thirsty and you gave me something to drink, I was a stranger and you invited me in, I needed clothes and you clothed me, I was sick and you looked after me, I was in prison and you came to visit me." Then the righteous will answer him, "Lord, when did we see you hungry and fee you, or thirsty and give you something to drink? When did we see you a stranger and invite you in, or needing clothes and clothe you? When did we see you sick or in prison and go to visit you?" The King will reply, "I tell you the truth, whatever you did for one of the least of these brothers of mine, you did for me."[169]

I find it humbling to consider the idea that I am God's representative: representing his very presence. But I am also aware of the fact, that the person in front of me represents Christ.

The giving Christ in me, ministers to the needy Christ in them. And there is the sense that the needy Christ in them, gives back to me–circular. The Lord is close to the brokenhearted through us. He ministers to the crushed in spirit through us. And at the same time, he is the brokenhearted and the crushed in spirit. At different times, we find ourselves representing the needy side of Jesus, on the receiving end of his love and grace as someone else speaks to us in the name of the Lord, as his representative.

In hospice, it seems that there is a period of time when people who are dying have one foot in this natural world and one foot in the spiritual world. During this period of time, which might be hours or days or weeks, they are often able to see and talk to angels, and see and talk to friends and relatives who have already died. I have come to believe that everyone gets escorted. I believe this happens to help them be at peace with their death, and by hearing the stories, to bolster the faith of those left behind.

---

[169] Matt 25:35-40.

A patient of mine, Cathy, had face cancer and half her face was missing – the whole right side. Her right eye, part of her nose, the cheek bones down to part of her lips had been removed. Awkward band aids covered open holes and oozing wounds, and the cancer continued its relentless destruction, evidenced by new outbreaks and holes. She talked with great difficulty. She told me that an angel came to visit her in the evening and always stood on the right side of her bed. She asked, "Do you believe me?" After a short pause, I said, "Of course I believe you. The angel is a spiritual person, and you are seeing it with your spiritual eyes which are working just fine." She died a few days later.

There is something about suffering that seems to draw the real presence of God down; that seems to make prayers more powerful and somehow more heard, if that's possible. That in our pain and suffering, we are better able to grab hold of the throne of grace or the hem of his garment, as God tells us, "I am close. I have drawn near to the brokenhearted and the crushed in spirit." One way I would define sacred is the giving Christ in me ministering to the needy Christ in you.

## ETHICS IN CHAPLAIN LEADERSHIP

General Bernard W. Rogers, Army Chief of Staff in 1977 said, "Chaplains have looked after the Army's spiritual welfare, have championed our soldiers' human needs, have set the moral tone for the Army. . . . They have always been there when we needed them."[170]

Ethics is an important part of most chaplaincy ministry and being able to understand and articulate ethical concepts is important. An ethical dilemma is when either of two positions on an issue seem to be right–the best of two rights. Likewise, the opposite would be the lesser of two evils. The chaplain is often looked to for guidance

---

[170] Brinsfield, *Encouraging Faith*, 62.

and instruction in these cases, and in this light can be a powerful leader in determining the best course of action.[171]

## LESSER OF TWO EVILS

Perhaps because of the horrors of World War I, before World War II a pacifist movement swept through the church. But the Nazi elimination of the Jews and the Japanese suppression of missionaries and churches, led Christians in America to rethink the pacifist stance. After the Japanese bombed Pearl Harbor, the Methodist Church General Conference reversed their position on war and stated: "We are well within the Christian position when we assert the necessity of the use of military forces to resist an aggression which would overthrow every right which is held sacred by civilized men."[172] Resisting the evil regimes of Germany, Italy, and Japan as they sought to dominate the people of the world was seen as a lesser evil than the theological problems of war itself.

## BEST OF TWO RIGHTS

I want to review the Teri Shiavo case, to show how the ethical dilemma developed, and how people came to their various conclusions. While working in Renal Dialysis, Oncology, and Hospice, I have been exposed many times to similar situations and dilemmas.

At about 5:30 a.m. on February 25th, 1990, Teresa Marie Schiavo finished using the bathroom, then collapsed in the apartment hallway from cardiac arrest brought on by an eating disorder (bulimia), which caused hypkalemia (extremely low potassium in the

---

[171] Laurel Arthur Burton, ed., *Making Chaplaincy Work: Practical approaches*, (New York: Haworth Press, 1988), 4.
[172] Gushwa, *The Best and Worst of Times*, 4:96.

blood). Her collapse awakened her husband, Michael, who called her parents and 911.

Before the paramedics arrived, Terri's brain was deprived of oxygen, and she slipped into

a coma. At Humana Northside Hospital of St. Petersburg, Florida, she was intubated,

ventilated, given a tracheotomy, and a gastric feeding tube. Although she came out of the

coma two and a half months later, the damage to her brain was permanent.[173]

Over the next few years, Terri was admitted to different rehabilitation units in

Florida and had an experimental brain stimulation treatment at the University of

California, San Francisco. Also at this time, without objection of the Schindler family,

the court made Michael Schiavo Terri's guardian. In an effort to better care for Terri,

Michael attended nursing school and became a respiratory therapist and emergency room

nurse.

In 1992, Michael Schiavo brought a medical malpractice suit against the

obstetrician they were seeing for fertility treatments. The suit alleged that he should have

diagnosed the bulimic condition. The jury agreed and awarded $700,000 to Terri and

$300,000 to Michael. Terri's award was put into a trust fund by the court to manage her

care.

In 1998, Terri's primary care physicians, Dr. Jeffrey Karp and Dr. Victor

Gambone, determined Terri to be in an irreversible persistent vegetative state (PVS). In

2001, the court ordered an examination by Dr. Ron Cranford, a University of Minnesota

neurologist. He determined from CT scans that eighty percent of Terri's upper brain had

atrophied and had been replaced with spinal fluid, her lower brain was damaged, and only

---

[173] Wikipedia Encyclopedia, "Terri Schiavo," *Wikipedia Web.* http://www.en.wikipedia.org/wiki/Terri Schiavo (22 Oct 2006).

the brain stem was working, controlling the involuntary functions of breathing and heartbeat. There was no cognitive function and no EEG activity of the cerebral cortex.

The court battle between Michael Schiavo and the Schindler family began in 2002. Michael chose two doctors to testify about Terri's condition, the family chose two, and the court chose a fifth. The five doctors examined Terri's medical records, brain scans, the videos, and herself. Three doctors (both of Michael's doctors and the court-appointed doctor) said she was in a persistent vegetative state. The two doctors representing the Schindlers said Terri was in a minimally conscious state. Judge Greer ruled that Terri was in a PVS. The Schindlers took the case to the Second District Court of Appeals, who upheld Judge Greer's decision.

The Schindler family continued to lose every court case and removal of the feeding tube grew imminent. In an effort to save their daughter's life, they encouraged media attention and public debate, and Terri Schiavo entered the living rooms of millions of people worldwide.

In March 2005, Terri's feeding tube was removed. In response, the Schindlers found Neurologist Dr. William Cheshire Jr., of the Jacksonville Mayo Clinic, who visited with Terri for ninety minutes and determined that the PVS diagnosis might be wrong. He contacted Florida Adult Protective Services. Based on Dr. Cheshire's affidavit, Governor Jeb Bush got involved and tried to have Terri's feeding tube reinserted.

The Schindler family took four and a half hours of video and tried to make a case for the minimally conscious state by showing that Terri seemed aware of people and certain words and actions. From this video they created and released six video segments totaling four minutes, twenty seconds which showed Terri smiling and apparently responding to stimuli. This raised public awareness and enraged people around the world. Based on this short video, Terri's parents sued for the court to recognize the minimally conscious state and reinsert the feeding tube. Using only the evidence of the four minute segment, the Schindlers got thirty-three doctors, of which fifteen were neurologists, to state that Terri was not in a persistent vegetative state but was actually minimally conscious.

Despite the firestorm of media coverage, Terri's feeding tube was removed March 18th. Thirteen days after her feeding tube was removed, on March 31st, Terri went into cardiac arrest and died in the arms of her husband, Michael.

The Terri Schiavo case polarized Christians into three camps: Those convinced that it was wrong to let Terri Schiavo die; those who thought it was right to let her die; those who did not know what was right or wrong. People from all religious, political, and ethical views took opposing sides. While some Catholic Cardinals and Bishops spoke in favor of letting her die, Franciscan monks took the other side and were supporting and ministering to the Schindler family.

The followers of Hippocrates believed in patient-centered ethics and the sanctity of all life. They took an oath to do no harm. At the same time, naturalistic Greeks had a different point of view and based their conclusions on the quality of life and what could be seen and felt. Terminally ill patients were often helped to die to alleviate pain and suffering.[174] After over two thousand years, much of the modern debate over Terri Schiavo's fate centered around the same issues of sanctity of life versus quality of life.

---

[174] Gregory E. Pence, *Classic Cases in Medical Ethics: Accounts of cases that have shaped medical ethics, with philosophical, legal, and historical backgrounds* (New York: McGraw Hill, 1990), 11.

Another aspect of the modern debate is that Terri was kept alive artificially. Without the feeding tube, she would have died thirteen years before. If this accident had happened in a third-world country, she would have died when the accident happened.

How is death defined? For thousands of years, brain death meant that a person was not breathing and did not have a heartbeat. The Cognitive Criterion of brain death is based on the loss of reason, memory, and self-awareness. The Irreversibility Standard defines death as irreversible unconsciousness or being in a persistent vegetative state (PVS) for over one year.[175] St Joseph Medical Center in Tacoma, WA, for transplant purposes, has a working definition of death that states that a patient is determined to be brain dead if the doctors agree that the person will die within 48 hours after life support is removed.

Karen Quinlan was in a coma in 1975, and Nancy Cruzan was in a coma in 1983. Both women were in persistent vegetative states. Karen's parents did not want to remove her respirator, and Nancy's parents wanted to remove her feeding tube. Both cases were decided in the courts. The New Jersey Supreme Court ruled in favor of the Quinlan family, allowing the family of a dying incompetent patient to decide to let the patient die by disconnecting life support. Ten years after her accident, her respirator was removed and she died. Five months after the U.S. Supreme Court ruled in favor of the Cruzan family, Nancy Cruzan's feeding tube was removed, and she died.

Despite these cases, the debate has continued over if and when to forego extraordinary means of life support. Advance directives by the patient can unequivocally state their right to die by the withdrawal or forgoing of treatment, and at the same time be overruled by well-meaning, but misguided, family members. The lack of an advance

---

[175] Pence, *Classic Cases*, 45.

directive leaves family members with the chore of determining what their loved one might want if they could make the choice, and then honoring that.

## Two Positions

In the case of Terri Schiavo, Michael was both her husband and court-appointed legal guardian. He reiterated her desire to never be kept alive in a vegetative state. When competent medical authority determined that she was in a persistent vegetative state, with irreversible brain damage, and that legally binding, then Michael had the right to request removal of her feeding tube. Michael was acting from the quality of life (good of the patient) point of view. Michael would say that he was operating out of his love for Terri.

Terri's parents were operating more from an emotional point of view, in that they did not want their daughter to die, whatever her wishes, and whatever her quality of life. They invoked the sanctity of life view, believing that Terri's life should be prolonged at all costs to its natural conclusion, even if the word *natural* could be debated. This idea argues that all killing is wrong, no matter what the circumstances. They were further bolstered in their belief as Catholics, when many Catholic clergy and other Christians rallied to their cause. They did not have the legal authority or ultimate possibility of either winning the case or gaining control. It might be argued that their edited video segments of Terri were a desperate attempt to manipulate Christians, the media, and politicians into joining their emotionally charged view in an attempt to get control of their daughter's fate. Based on the video segments and conflicting expert opinion, none of these groups understood or believed the persistent vegetative state. The Schindlers would also argue that they were operating out of love for Terri.

Graded absolutism holds that some moral absolutes can come into conflict and moral laws are not all equal.[176] Jesus stated that there was a *greater commandment*, suggesting that not all moral laws have equal weight.[177] Graded absolutism is not to be confused with conflicting absolutism. Greater absolutism sees the greater good or highest obligation, while conflicting absolutism seeks the lesser of two evils. Evangelicals would argue that two moral absolutes cannot be in conflict.[178] Luther wrote that since Christians were members of both the kingdom of God and of this world, and with responsibilities in both, it was inevitable that conflicts would arise.[179] Although God's moral law is absolute, *the law of the Lord is perfect*, Jesus suggested that not all sins are equal, that there were lesser and greater sins, and there are higher and lower moral laws.[180] He said, "The one who handed me over to you is guilty of a greater sin."[181]

Using the idea of greater absolutism, is there ever an occasion when the quality of life is more important than the sanctity of life? Let's look at it another way. Which is more merciful–sanctity of life: to artificially prolong the life of a person who would otherwise die; or, quality of life: to allow the person to die naturally by stopping artificial treatments? Passive euthanasia might have an answer.

---

[176] Norman L. Geisler, *Christian Ethics: Options and Issues* (Grand Rapids: Baker Book House, 1989), 27.
[177] Matt 22:34-36.
[178] Geisler, *Christian Ethics*, 97.
[179] Geisler, *Christian Ethics*, 98.
[180] Psalm 19:7.
[181] John 19:11.

PASSIVE EUTHANASIA

Allowing someone to die a natural death by withholding water and food (unnatural

lifesaving mechanisms) is not always wrong. Intravenous feeding is unnatural, but it is

delivering food, which is a natural means of sustaining life. If a person is so brain

damaged that they cannot swallow, are we morally obligated to put a tube down their

throat or directly into their stomach to artificially prolong their life? I believe prolonging

life unnaturally is wrong when it interferes with the natural process of death, which God

has ordained. Genesis 2:16, Romans 5:12, and Psalms 90:10 state that God has appointed

all people to die and has set natural limits to life.

By putting a person on life support in an effort to save their life or possibly find a

cure, an ethical dilemma occurs when those efforts fail and the artificial means continues

to unnecessarily prolong the life, which would have ended naturally long before. In this

case, three criteria should be considered: (1) The disease or condition is irreversible and

cannot be corrected. There is no medical hope of recovery. (2) Patient veto power: The

patient has veto power over any decision not to extend life by artificial means. If the

patient is not conscious, their living will should be respected. In the absence of a will, the

person or people responsible for them must make the decision. (3) A collective decision:

Consider spiritual, legal, moral and family implications to a decision by consulting others

and getting consent from the pastor, doctor, lawyer, and family members.[182]

The principle of *benefit versus burden* is often used to determine a course of

action. It amounts to drawing a line down the middle of the page, creating two columns,

benefit and burden, and looking at all options for the patient in relation to these.

Depending on the weight given a particular benefit or burden, people of good will may

---

[182] Geisler, *Christian Ethics*, 168-9.

132

still come to different conclusions. In that case, the presence and help from the chaplain can be invaluable.

Christians should serve God, not play God. If God is sovereign over life, then treatment should be voluntary, improve life, and work in cooperation with the natural course of life as God has ordained it. There is no divine duty to unnaturally prolong human life.[183] Christian ethics are based on the love of God and love for others as the greatest commandment.[184] If sins of omission are as wrong as sins of commission, then we do not have a moral duty to prolong life unnecessarily if it just prolongs death.[185] The application of these principles determines our responsibility and direction, and informs the chaplain leader when facilitating discussions about what actions to take.

Understanding ethics is important wherever a chaplain works. In my personal experience, hospice, oncology, and renal dialysis, patients and family members struggle with the idea of quality of life versus quantity of life every day. My first patient in the renal dialysis clinic, on my very first day, was a 50 year old woman who told me she was thinking about stopping the three-times-a-week dialysis treatments because she was so miserable. We talked a long time about quantity versus quality of life. We talked about her poor self image, her view of God who was far away and not particularly present, and what, in her present life, gave her joy and love. It was a fruitful discussion. She agreed to meet me every Thursday afternoon to discuss these things. This appointment gave her something to look forward to all week, and we made wonderful progress in all of these areas, and she found meaning in her life and reasons to keep living.

---

[183] Geisler, *Christian Ethics*, 183.
[184] Matt 22:37-39.
[185] James 4:17.

A hospice patient of mine, a Baptist minister and social work counselor, left clearly written instructions stating that he did not want to live or be kept alive if his Parkinson's disease reduced him to a persistent vegetative state. Over a period of five years, the disease slowly but relentlessly progressed. Finally, he declined into the vegetative state he most feared, receiving his liquids and food through a tube. After three months, his wife painfully decided to honor his final wishes. This meant that his food and water would stop, and he would slowly starve to death. The doctor had to approve the decision, and he did. The nursing facility said they would comply with the doctor's order, although some nurses, who had been treating the patient, were not happy about it. I honored his decision and supported his wife in her vigil. She sat by his bedside every day, singing hymns, reading to him, and praying, and I did the same thing once or twice a week, also supporting the staff. Over a two week period, he did not receive water or food and slowly declined until he died.

## Jonseniand Paradigm

Dr. Albert R. Jonsen, Ph.D., Professor Emeritus of Ethics at the University of

Washington School of Medicine, Seattle, Washington, developed this formula for

determining, analyzing, and resolving clinical ethical problems. The goal is to find a

balanced judgment that meets the care needs of the patient, when they find themselves in

a dilemma as to which course of action to take.

Whether a chaplain in a hospital or a pastor in the local church, ethical issues and

problems come up that must be worked through. A church member might want to know

what the pastor thinks about continuing dialysis treatments given their poor quality of life

and declining health. Another member might want to forego chemo therapy in hopes that

God will heal them of their cancer. In the hospital, doctors might suggest to family

members that the ventilation machine be turned off, since they can do no more for the

patient who is sure to die.

The basic structure of the model consists of four areas: Medical Indications (the

patient's medical context), Quality of Life, Patient Preferences, and Contextual Features

(other circumstances: family, religion, finances, culture, influences). Each area has one or

more of the following moral principles associated with it: Patient Autonomy (the patient

makes decisions about their care and treatment), Beneficence (assist and benefit patient),

Nonmaleficence (cause no harm), and Justice (do what's right).

Appendix B shows the chart with its four pieces, as developed by Dr. Jonsen, and

I have included more questions and comments in each area to assist in using it.[186] The

key people involved in the patient's welfare (the patient, family, doctor(s), nurse(s),

---

[186] Albert R. Jonsen, Mark Siegler, and William J. Winslade, *Clinical Ethics: A practical approach to ethical decisions in clinical medicine*, 6 ed. (New York: McGraw-Hill, 2006), 11.

chaplain/clergy) should meet to discuss the care options using this diagram. In some instances, the hospital ethics committee looks at a case using this formula to see if they can recommend a course of treatment for a doctor, or to review a decision already made.

Even with the diagram and the questions, there are almost innumerable variations and possibilities, because each case is unique as each person is unique. Ultimately, the patient has the final say, within limits (Doctors are not obligated to follow the patient's wishes, if they contradict the goals of the medicine).

To use the chart, someone from the group draws a large plus sign on the board to indicate the four boxes. Starting with the upper left box, questions around the medical aspects of the patient's situation (Medical Indications) are reviewed, and the answers are written in that part of the box.

| Medical Indications | Patient Preferences |
|---|---|
| Quality of Life | Contextual Features |

Jonseniand Clinical Ethics Diagram.

Then questions about quality of life, patient preference, and contextual features, are answered and written in the appropriate spaces. When all of the questions are answered, and other questions thought up at the time, an answer may start to present itself. Even then it might be hard to make a decision. It takes everyone working together to reach a decision, and in most cases, for the patient's sake sooner is better than later.

When a decision has been made (or if a decision isn't exactly presenting itself), it is important to ensure the patient is fully informed of all options, opinions, and anything else crucial to the making of a decision. When all is said and done, it is important for everyone to respect and honor the patient's decision.

For a detailed analysis and discussion of this formula, with numerous examples, I recommend the book, *Clinical Ethics*, already referenced here, by Albert R. Jonsen, Mark Siegler, and William J. Winslade.

## ETHICS IN THE MILITARY

Chaplains are supposed to consider ethics in all situations, and they are required to speak up if they see ethical injustice. Chaplain Orris E. Kelly, Chief of Chaplains in the Army from 1975 to 1979 wrote: "We ought to be the definers and proclaimers of ethics and morality. . . . I believe we should be committed to help create within the Army an atmosphere of ethical and moral consideration based on personal integrity which facilitates responsibility."[187]

As moral relativism swept through theological circles and colleges, Chaplain Kermit D. Johnson, Chief of Chaplains from 1979 to 1982, wrote to the Dean of Harvard Divinity School:

> The whole ethical area is so very important. So many matters of life and death are before us precisely at a time when theological and philosophical bases have been so thoroughly eroded, that few dare speak with any authority. I personally believe

---

[187] Brinsfield, *Encouraging Faith*, 6:67.

that unless universals exist, we have absolutely no basis for making ethical judgments and everything is up for grabs.[188]

Chaplain Johnson believed that ethics proceeded from a grounding in faith, and because of that, chaplains were in a unique position to help guide the military.

On August 12, 1949, in Geneva, Switzerland, the rules for victims of war was adopted as the standard for humane treatment in the world. The meeting was called the *Diplomatic Conference for the Establishment of International Conventions for the Protection of Victims of War*.[189] The document consisted of one hundred, forty-three Articles outlining how prisoners would be treated. It was written in English and French, sent to the United Nations, and almost all countries sent written agreement to follow its precepts. In this section, I want to look at chaplains as noncombatants and torture.

Chaplains are considered noncombatants. Geneva Convention, Protocol I, Article 43.2 states that chaplains do not participate in combat; hence, noncombatants. But Protocol I, Art 13.2(a) does allow for them to carry weapons with permission, typically from their commanding officer. British chaplains were armed at times during WWII, and in Vietnam some chaplains carried an M16 rifle while patrolling with the soldiers they served. In accordance the Geneva Convention, Third Convention, Chapter IV, Art 33, captured chaplains are not considered enemy combatants and can be returned to their country or choose to stay to aid other prisoners.

---

[188] Brinsfield, *Encouraging Faith*, 6:133.
[189] Office of the United Nations High Commissioner for Human Rights Geneva, Switzerland, "Geneva Convention Relative to the Treatment of Prisoners of War," 2006. *Geneva Convention Web.* http://www.unhchr.ch/html/menu3/b/91.htm (22 Oct 2006).

What would happen if a country decided to reinterpret the Geneva Convention articles to suit their own perceived needs? The issue becomes an ethical dilemma when people in charge seek to modify its precepts to meet their own needs and agenda. Using the ethical argument, *the end justifies the means*, President George W. Bush decided to use torture to elicit desired information from Taliban prisoners about other possible attacks on the United States. Senator John McCain and former Secretary of State Colin Powell spoke out against this move and philosophy. McCain had been a prisoner of war in Vietnam, so he was personally sensitive to the issue. The Washington Post reported, "Joining McCain and the other Republicans this week was former secretary of state Colin L. Powell, who wrote in a letter that reinterpreting the Geneva Conventions would encourage other countries to 'doubt the moral basis of our fight against terrorism.' "[190]

As a chaplain in the military or serving with a military service organization, like the Veterans of Foreign Wars or the American Legion, issues of lawful orders, moral dilemmas, and human rights could swirl around your ministry. What do you say? When do you speak up? How do you speak up?

As a chaplain and retired Army officer, I am concerned. There are many ways to get involved, and being aware of the issue and the debate is a first step. Voting and writing our elected officials is another. In my own case, I agree with Senator McCain that there is no provision for reinterpreting the Geneva Convention articles. Although it might be harder to keep the country secure, in my opinion, the torture of prisoners of war is never an option.

---

[190] Peter Baker, "GOP Infighting on Detainees Intensifies Bush Threatens to Halt CIA Program if Congress Passes Rival Proposal," 2006. *Washington Post Web.* http://www.washingtonpost.com/wp-dyn/content/article/2006/09/15/AR2006091500483.html (16 Oct 2006).

Jesus told his disciples, "And I will do whatever you ask in my name, so that the Son may bring glory to the Father."[191] Some people believe that there is only one way to pray, and so we have this story, "A military jury today convicted a Navy chaplain of a misdemeanor count of disobeying his commanding officer for wearing his uniform while delivering a prayer "in Jesus" name" at an assembly in front of the White House."[192]

The Navy Chaplain Office told chaplains, that when dressed in their uniform, to not end public prayers with *in Jesus' name*. In a sign of the times, they felt that a public audience, not a denominational church service, could represent different faiths, and they did not want those people to possibly be offended. A spokesperson for the Navy Chaplain Office said, "Navy chaplains are encouraged to be sensitive to the needs of all those present," she said, "and may decline an invitation to pray if not able to do so for conscience reasons."[193]

I am not saying the Navy Chaplain Office decision is right; I'm just reporting what they decided. Recently, a military chaplain was court-martialed, because he insisted that all of his prayers must end in Jesus' name, no matter where they took place, no matter how he was dressed, and he did so in defiance of his direct orders.

In the chaplaincy ministry, there are times when it is necessary to compromise on the practice of the ministry, but not on what you believe. It is an essential part of the training for ministry and the ministry itself that the chaplain be able and willing to serve all people–period. If I am ministering to Buddhist, Jewish, or Muslim patients, I do not

---

[191] John 14:13.

[192] World Net Daily, "Faith Under Fire: Chaplain who prayed in Jesus' name convicted. Klingenschmitt jury now will consider punishment," 2006. *World Net Daily Web.* http://www.wnd.com/news/article.asp?ARTICLE_ID=51973 (23 Oct 2006).

[193] Julia Duin, "Military chaplains told to shy from Jesus," 2005. *The Washington Times Web.* http://www.washtimes.com/national/20051221-121224-6972r.htm (22 Oct 2006).

force my religion on them or try to proselytize them. I want to help them in their suffering and meet them where they are at.

Chaplain (Lt) Gordon James Klingenschmitt was convicted by court-martial on September 13, 2006, and after the hearing he said, "There is no more fundamental right than the inalienable right to worship our creator, and I pray in Jesus name," He went on to say, "For any government official to require non-sectarian prayers is for him to enforce his government religion upon me, to censor, exclude, and punish me for my participation."

I understand where Chaplain Klingenschmitt is coming from, and I respect his decision to make a stand on an issue important to him. I also understand what the office of chaplain means, and what is expected in that ministry. While taking the risk of sounding heretical to some, I have to disagree with Chaplain Klingenschmitt, because I feel he has taken a narrow view of his chaplaincy ministry. In this particular case, I would work for a change in this policy, but I would not disobey the direct order to make my point. Perhaps, it is a matter of faith.

If ending my prayer a certain way offends people, I am happy to change that, because it is not about me, it is about them and about God. My prayer is no less powerful or less effective. If I believe my prayer is less effective or ineffective because I left out those three words, *in Jesus' name*, then I lack faith, and I limit God's response to my prayers based on a formula. All of my prayers are in Jesus' name, whether I say the *magic* words or not, because to begin with, I pray in faith believing that God, in Jesus' name, answers all of my prayers anyhow. Why else would I pray? I pray absolutely knowing I am heard and expecting an answer every time.

And if the person I am ministering to, lying in bed dying of cancer, asks me about my hope, my God, my faith, my beliefs, I am prepared to give an answer. I am open to that. I hope for that. "But in your hearts set apart Christ as Lord. Always be prepared to give an answer to everyone who asks you to give the reason for the hope that you have. But do this with gentleness and respect."[194] Like Peter wrote, I treat them with respect, ready to give an answer. But until then, I meet them in their suffering and help them find comfort, healing, and reconciliation.

In conclusion, I like what Chaplain Jesse L. Thornton had to say about the military chaplaincy: "Chaplains are God's constant reminder among us of his care for us all. That is why, on the battlefield, chaplains must be at the right place and at the right time–with soldiers–for ministry."[195] Let me paraphrase this: Chaplains are God's constant reminder among us of his care for us all. That is why, wherever God has called us to serve, if we are willing to submit ourselves to God and serve where called, chaplains will be at the right place and right time for ministry.

RELIGIOUS TOLERANCE

In fundamental and evangelical circles, tolerance is often seen as a dirty word. It means that the Gospel has been compromised in order to minister to all people, and what results is a washed out, flavorless, meaningless ministry that has no power to change lives or more importantly save souls. But nothing could be further from the truth.

Religious tolerance does not mean that we give up our own beliefs and practices. It does not mean that we compromise our beliefs in the function of the ministry, and it

---

[194] I Peter 3:15.
[195] Brinsfield, Jr., *Encouraging Faith*, 81.

does not mean we have to accept as true what the other person believes in order to minister to them.

Religious tolerance means you respect the beliefs of other people. As a chaplain called to minister to all people, the first priority is to let people be themselves and express or explore their personal spiritual and religious beliefs. The chaplain facilitates and encourages this sharing as a way of experiencing the person as a person. People want to tell their story, they want to be heard, and when they are in great need, they want to be experienced by people who care.

Why would you be there as a chaplain? In most cases, you would be there because the person has a great need. It is, first, a time of empathetic listening and caring. The chaplain wants to help that person find peace and hope in a difficult situation, and knowing what the other person believes helps the chaplain minister to them in a way that brings familiarity and comfort.

Proselytizing is forbidden. If a person feels compelled at all times to convert others to their faith, then they should not be a chaplain. If a patient in the hospital asks about the chaplain's faith, the chaplain can share what they believe and why, but the purpose of the sharing is not to induce someone to convert. Proselytizing is often grounds for dismissal.

# CHAPTER 7 – CHAPLAINS AT WORK AND IN LEADERSHIP

Chaplains serve in facilities and situations that bring them into contact with people in need and in crisis. The type of crisis is unique to each person, even if they are in beds next to each other and suffering from the same disease. In this section, I want to look at some of the ministry challenges, and those tools for working and coping with those challenges. Leadership challenges, spiritual assessment, theological reflection, and disenfranchised grief cover some of the important aspects of this ministry.

The leadership challenges section is a sort of *in the trenches* look at the chaplain's ministry, and how those challenges were addressed. Spiritual assessment is a quick, easy to learn method of determining the person's spiritual needs, which helps the chaplain meet the person's needs at a basic level. The theological reflection section is about how theological reflection can help a chaplain determine a patient's deeper needs, reflect on an encounter with a patient, and cope with the unique stresses associated with this ministry. Finally, a thorough understanding of disenfranchised grief is important for understanding the dynamics of suffering and the emotional issues that might lie under the surface of a suffering person, and which might even be driving the disease process.

Wherever I worked in the hospital or hospice, I provided pastoral care to people experiencing loss and grief. In rehabilitation many of my patients were struggling with how to look at their life and find meaning after a stroke. All of my patients in the mental health unit were struggling with coping through losses and griefs of some kind. In oncology loss and grief were, at times, almost palpable. My very first patient in renal dialysis said she wanted to turn off the dialysis machine because the quantity of her poor life was not as important as the quality she had lost. Another dialysis patient was a former athlete who suffered with the side effects of diabetes.

One of my patients, mentioned earlier, wanted to stop dialysis. She had only been on dialysis for three months, she had diabetes and had lost her kidneys due to drug abuse. In our visits, we talked about what gave her life meaning, and we made an agreement to meet every Thursday when she came in. This gave us a short-term goal, and she told me many times that she looked forward to our Thursday afternoon visits. It was hard for her to understand and internalize that she had personal value, that God really loved her, or that someone cared for her. She had huge loss and grief issues from a life of sexual and drug abuse. Together we grappled with all of this.

Another patient, a middle aged man, was a football star in high school and college. Now his toes and parts of his feet have been amputated and parts of his hands. Diabetes was taking his body a piece at a time, and his wounds were not healing. He struggled to find hope and purpose in his debilitating disease. His mom had a reoccurrence of her pancreatic cancer and at the time had only four to six weeks to live.

As she struggled with her cancer in the hospital, I visited her each day and tried to bring comfort and reassurance to her family and her son.

Visiting her seemed to open up my ministry. Her son had been on dialysis for many years, and his mom had been active in church and in visiting other patients in dialysis. As I spent time with her, her friends came up after finishing dialysis, but her pastor had not come to visit. Although she learned he was not feeling well, she was angry and sad. I reminded her that I was her pastor's representative, that in his illness I was there as an extension of his ministry. She accepted that, and suddenly I found that my ministry in dialysis had blossomed. I was seeing more people, more often, because they were friends of this woman. They saw my care for her, and we all became acquainted. I was adopted into the dialysis community.

One thing I learned was that everyone sees dialysis differently. It might be life saving to one and a chance at a second life, but with another person it is a burden that is endured for as long as they can tolerate it, and then they give it up, either intentionally or by non-compliance (don't follow strict food and liquid restrictions, stop taking medications, miss a few treatments here and there).

Many times I was very impressed with the wonderful attitude people had, when their circumstances would have warranted something other. I met people who were on dialysis because of mistakes doctors made in medications, yet after a period of anger, they found a reason to laugh. Many patients had multiple amputations, some with stubs for arms and legs, yet they persevered and were an inspiration to others. Some patients were in such dire straights financially, that they trembled in fear of what lurked around the corner. Then there were those who were going to die in a few weeks; they knew it, the doctors and nurses knew it, we all knew it. And we would sit with them, hold their hand, and talk–sometimes about nothing at all, sometimes about everything.

I also conducted the loss and grief group on the Mental Health unit. Although the teaching was mostly educational in nature; nevertheless, people experiencing great losses and deep griefs encountered one another. Each group seemed to go in its own direction, and sometimes it filled me with a little anxiety. But it always seemed to work out. People shared their experiences and stories, and we talked about good coping and not so good coping, and patients and staff said they found the group helpful.

Chaplaincy must include inclusivity and diversity as foundational values, or chaplains will fail in their ministry to meet those people they are called to help. Recognizing and honoring the person's religion, faith, group, race, ethnicity, sexual orientation, gender, age, and disability, means that no one is left behind. Recognizing, honoring, and affirming this freedom, not imposing their own beliefs, gives chaplains the perspective of a true servant.

In addition, proselytizing is a breach of ethics and is expressly forbidden in professional chaplaincy. It does not mean that a chaplain compromises what they believe, but it does mean that the other person can be ministered to without compromising their beliefs or with the fear that you, the chaplain, have an ulterior motive. If you think that your chaplaincy ministry is about you, then you will be worried about compromising what you believe. If the ministry is about the other person, you will meet them where they are at, not trying to change them to fit your mold or idea of religion. In the end, it is not about compromise, it is about respect and reverence and compassion.

Chaplains who feel compelled to share their faith with others, must keep this desire in check, unless they come from the same faith tradition of the person, or the person wants to hear about their faith. "Preach the gospel at all times, and if necessary, use words." Francis of Assisi is not the author of this saying, although he said words similar to this, and it has a decidedly *Franciscan* flavor.[196] But the statement rings true, because Jesus talked about letting our light shine before people, and James talked about faith requiring actions, and hearing requiring deeds.[197] In other words, live your faith, trust that God has put you in this position, and if someone asks about your faith, be prepared to answer.

Chaplain Carey H. Cash was the chaplain for a Marine battalion in the first days of the attack on Iraq in 2003. In the opening remarks of his book, *A Table in the Presence*, Chaplain Cash writes: "As a chaplain to a battalion of front-line combat Marines, I had the unique privilege of witnessing firsthand how God miraculously delivered and even transformed the lives of men confronted with the terrors of war."[198] He goes on to describe, in a vivid dramatic detail, how the lives of his men were transformed by humility, faith, and prayer, and at times by the apparent miraculous intervention of God, where many of them should have died.

In one part, after they had already sustained casualties, he prayed with the men before they went back out. "When our time for prayer was over and it was time for the AAV to pull out, I tried, as best I could, to lay my hands on each one of them, on an arm,

---

[196] E.M. Almedingen, *St. Francis of Assisi: A great life in brief* (New York: Barnes & Noble Books, 1967), 89.
[197] Matt 5:16, James 2:17, 1:22.
[198] Carey H. Cash, *A Table in the Presence*, (Nashville: W Publishing, 2004), xii.

a shoulder, or a hand. Human touch, I found, became an all-important symbol to them, nearly sacramental in its import."[199]

As mentioned before, the work of the Holy Spirit can be circular, with the minister blessing people and the people blessing the minister. Like all ministers, Christian chaplains also struggle to be the representative of Jesus Christ: his hands, his eyes, his voice. In this section, Cash talks about what his ministry felt like and how it blessed him.

"Marines expect their chaplains to inspire them, and of course I hope and pray that I did that. But it was the men's humble love for God and simple faith in His power to heal, forgive, and protect, that became a source of unspeakable blessing for me in my own walk with Christ."[200] The book recounts many stories of faith and how everyone supported each other in the face of insurmountable odds and the horrors of war. The work of chaplains takes them where the need is greatest, often as this book describes, at the peril of their own lives.

## SPIRITUAL ASSESSMENT

Spiritual assessment is about determining the patient's support system, coping abilities, and relationships with a higher power, themselves, and others. Spiritual assessment is important to the work of chaplaincy, if the chaplain is going to be a spiritual leader in the lives of their people. How well this is accomplished can determine the outcome of the ministry and has a direct effect on their ability to lead.

---

[199] Cash, *Table in the Presence*, 121.
[200] Cash, *Table in the Presence*, 129.

A common lament among people trying to understand and sort out the many definitions of spirituality is how diverse and yet distinct they seem to be. Buddhist, Shaman, New Age, Christian, American Indian, naturalist, agnostic and many others describe an awareness and experience that transcends religion, self, and other: something that speaks to the deeper interconnectiveness of all things, in all things, flowing outward into all things. Fundamentally, spirituality is about relations and relationships.

The concept of spirituality addresses the human need to believe in or embrace something greater than ourselves, to address an inner emptiness, feelings of unfulfillment, and questions about the presence of evil, suffering, meaning of life, the meaning of things, and death and dying.

Using the concept of *upward, inward, outward*, we can find a common thread of understanding in the idea of spirituality in all things, and a fairly easy formula for doing a spiritual assessment. The following is an all-encompassing definition of spirituality: *Spirituality is upward, inward, and outward aspects of a relationship and connection to something "other" than our selves.*

*Other* can be described as God, Jesus, Father, Mother, Buddha, Krishna, Goddess, the Divine, Nothingness, Sacredness, Perfection, Beauty including anything higher or greater or deeper than our personal self, which brings fulfillment, peace, calmness, peaceful consciousness, enlightenment, inner stability, awareness at all or many levels, and on a more practical note, better coping skills, and perhaps improved health.

To do a spiritual assessment, we could ask the person specific and probing questions: How is spirituality or religion important to you and how you cope? What church or spiritual support community helps you? What spiritual or religious questions

150

concern you? What beliefs do you have that might impact your care?[201] If the patient is not particularly religious, asking questions that determine how they cope with illness, what gives them meaning and purpose, what beliefs might impact their care, and what family and social resources support them provide the same types of answers.[202]

Over the course of the pastoral visit, through their story telling and attentive listening, answers to the following questions will present themselves automatically, based on the upward, inward, outward definition above.

## Upward Relationship

Do you believe in or have a connection or relationship with something larger, greater or higher than yourself? What is your relation to this something? Are you aware of a spiritual meaning or purpose of life?

The connection might be experienced as wonder, awe, reverence, a sense of being anchored, a sense of being loved, a sense of being found, peacefulness, peaceful darkness, a sense of floating, a sense of other. The relationship might be expressed in prayer, meditation, silence, chanting, quietness, reflection, contemplation, upward focus, upward looking. Hoping to not sound conflicted, it also can be a deep inward focus, such as a sense of *centeredness* within the body.

Linda was in her second round of chemotherapy and was responding well to treatment. When she talked of her reverence and love for nature and her dogs, she seemed to glow. Being in nature, working to preserve its sanctity, and spending time with her animals gave her life meaning and purpose and filled a need inside her.

---

[201] Harold G. Koenig, *Spirituality in Patient Care: Why, how, when, and what* (Philadelphia: Templeton Foundation, 2002), 22.
[202] Koenig, *Spirituality in Patient Care*, 23.

When people *look* upward, it is with the hope and expectation that a relationship is possible; that it is possible to *touch* that something greater, deeper, and other than ourselves. The upward aspect carries with it the idea of the person searching, and at the same time the anticipation of finding and establishing that connection. We could then conclude that many people in the world and over the centuries would not continue to seek without some form of spiritual feedback.

Simultaneously, the upward brings us a sense of being below, individual and unique; that the *other* is higher or greater or deeper. Looking for that *something* can be a life long journey. Finding that something can be an existential awakening, expanded consciousness, religious ecstasy, and the transcendental experience that makes life on this planet worth living and brings understanding and meaning.

Conflict in this area can be manifested as a questioning attitude, sense of something missing or unperceived loss, restlessness, a sense of unfulfillment despite secular and religious accomplishments. Also, something like chronic pain can inextricably replace the original upward relationship.[203]

INWARD RELATIONSHIP

Does your belief bring you hope, calm, peace, assurance, love? The inward aspect speaks of the spiritual self, identity, balance and insight and is the result of a personal belief system. It asks the questions, "Who am I? What am I? What is my purpose? The inward is expressed as devotion, inward faith, forgiveness, gentleness, self-love, personal insight, self-determination, and personal growth.

---

[203] Paul W. Pruyser, *The Minister as Diagnostician: Personal problems in pastoral perspective* (Louisville: Westminster John Knox Press, 1976), 118-122.

152

The inward speaks to the emptying of your self. Thomas Moore wrote, "Spiritual emptiness doesn't lead to resignation or depression; on the contrary, it gives hope and frees us from the anxiety of having to be in control. Emptiness is the very essence of religion and the spiritual life. . . . It is the pristine condition of the soul and the prerequisite for glimpsing the divine."[204]

If this area is in conflict, it is manifested as feelings of fear, guilt, anxiety, depression, ambivalence, anger, confusion, criticism, defensiveness, pride, powerlessness, loneliness, shame, and unresolved issues. The struggle here is between head and heart, working out the upward and inward relationship based on their personal belief system.

Michael told me he could not forgive himself for the mistakes he had made in life. Although he attended a local Baptist church regularly and knew in his head that God forgave him, he didn't believe he was worthy of forgiveness. The guilt, anger, and depression he felt inside left him with a sense of despair. When his renal dialysis treatment required his cooperation, his efforts were half-hearted and the staff was worried about him. Our first visits centered on his upward relationship and what he understood of it. I noticed the disparity between what he knew in his head and what he felt in his heart: Who was God to him? What was his concept of God? During our time together and his own discovery, his *Mount Olympus* idea of God changed to an intimate father/son–father/child relationship, and he was able to find the forgiveness he desperately craved. His dialysis treatment stabilized.

---

[204] Thomas Moore, *The Soul's Religion* (New York: HarperCollins), 13-15.

How does your belief affect your life in community? This relationship has an action element and focus towards community and/or nature. The outward relationship is demonstrated in fellowship, service, compassion, loving and being loved, forgiving and being forgiven, mercy, celebration, sacrament, and ritual. Wayne Muller wrote, "Clearly our sense of who we are is powerfully influenced by the community from which we come. [They] exert tremendous influence over the way we come to see ourselves."[205]

The absence of connection is experienced as loneliness, disconnection, abandonment, being adrift, *going it alone*, lack of support, disaffection, and disenfranchisement, and anxiety.

For clarification, the outward aspect could be further divided into two categories: Interpersonal (People Partnering) and Communapersonal (Communal Partnering). Interpersonal focuses on romantic love, parenting, childing, friending, learning, elders, siblings, grandparenting, help getting and help giving. Communapersonal focuses on family of origin, cultural community, neighborhood, gender community, peer community, faith community, nation, human community, citizenship, and athletic community.[206]

Disenfranchised grief could be defined as the severing of an outward relationship. I have had patients who were disenfranchised when their loved one died. In several cases, they were living with someone although not married, and the family excluded them from

---

[205]Wayne Muller, *How Then Shall We Live? Four simple questions that reveal the beauty and meaning of our lives* (New York: Bantam Books, 1997), 41.
[206] Gordon J. Hilsman, *Primary Spiritual Arenas* (Unpublished paper: Used by permission).

the funeral. The inability to attend the funeral and grieve in public left them disconnected, broken-hearted, and feeling abandoned.

There is a certain flow in the relationships of these three aspects of the spiritual self. When an upward relationship is recognized and developed, it affects, even creates or makes possible an inward relationship. A person's faith in God, for example, can be experienced as an inward sense of peace and hope. As this aspect of the relationship grows, it is often manifested outwardly in relations with people or creation around them. I am reminded of Saint Francis, whose deep and profound love of God was manifested in love and service to others, and connection to the natural world. The American Indians have a profound understanding of the connection between The Great Spirit, creation, and their place and role within it, which is then understood as interconnectiveness.

Henri J. Nouwen said it this way,

> When we are not afraid to enter into our own center and to concentrate on the stirrings of our own soul, we come to know that being alive means being loved. This experience tells us that we can only love because we are born out of love, that we can only give because our life is a gift, and that we can only make others free because we are set free by Him whose heart is greater than ours.[207]

Do you see the three elements of spirituality in this paragraph? Henri said we receive a gift from him whose heart is greater than ours. We enter into our own center to concentrate on the stirrings of our own soul. And this is expressed in service to others– making others free.

This three-part relationship has a natural, holistic flow. The upward, inward, and outward spiritual dimension is three-dimensional and flows in all directions back and through each aspect. We receive from God by the Holy Spirit, give something back in prayer, and give something to others. We learn about something inside us and convey that

---

[207] Nouwen, *Wounded Healer*, 91.

back to God and to others. Who we are is influenced by our community, by the Lord, and how we come to understand this work. Others share their experience, provide feedback, or provide the opportunity for reflection on our ministry to them, and it touches us inside, and is expressed in thankfulness and awe to God and so flows out to the others–reciprocal, dynamic, fluid, flowing.

There is a sense of personal growth. A sense of growing closer. And it seems at times to carry a certain expectation–perhaps anticipation. Moses wanted to see the face of God. For Moses that was the ultimate moment: to put a face on the one who was speaking to him. Moses stood on a rock, and as God passed by, he put Moses into the cleft of the rock and covered him with his hand. Moses saw just a glimpse of the living God as he passed, and only from behind, yet the people at the bottom of the mountain reported that he was glowing, and he had to cover his face with a veil.[208]

If a person gets stuck (fixed or focused primarily) in the upward or first aspect of the relationship, we hear the term, *so heavenly minded that they are of no earthly good.* One might have a sense of rapture, but it is not expressed or experienced as a personal benefit to themselves or to others. If the focus remains inward with no outward expression, we can become very spiritual, but people, nature, and community seldom benefit–hermits hiding in caves. Likewise, an exclusively outward focus often leaves the busy person temporarily satisfied but empty and dry inside.

Life is about coping with the necessary transitions, losses, guilts, and regrets. When the chaplain visits someone, discerning their spiritual needs and assessing their spirituality has a direct effect on their future health and medical outcomes. Chaplains often hear accounts of regrets, failed coping, and the results of transitions not well

---

[208] Exod 33:18-23, 34:29-35.

negotiated. We learn from the terminally ill that unresolved personal conflicts can fill them with a great fear of dying.[209] The chaplain can help lead them through this quagmire.

It is important to not judge or even anticipate what the spiritual assessment outcome will be before doing it. The person's spirituality may not meet our expectations, but be just as powerful for them. Henry Nouwen wrote, "Anyone who wants to pay attention without intention has to be at home in his own house–that is, he has to discover the center of his life in his own heart. Concentration, which leads to meditation and contemplation, is therefore the necessary precondition for true hospitality."[210] As caregivers, finding our own balance in the three relationships allows a more intuitive, open, and more effective approach to all types of ministry. Knowing how we live with these relationships allows us to lead others.

One technique for making an assessment is to sit down with someone and explore current and past relationships – a life review, their history, their story. "What was it like growing up without a father. . . ." If they are not particularly spiritual or aware of spirituality, the best place to start is with their family, community relations, or work. In other words, start with the third aspect, the outward, and work your way up.

If family and community relationships seem strong, turn inward. This is the realm of sin, guilt, disenfranchisement, suffering, and pain. They may be *bothered* about something that is difficult, if not impossible, for them to express. Beginning with a gentle statement like, "You seem to have a burden on your heart", coming alongside another in their confusion, suffering and pain, with attention and love, will help coax this to the

---

[209] Callanan, *Final Gifts*, 141-172.
[210] Nouwen, *Wounded Healer*, 90.

surface. Let them talk. Listen attentively. Look for the broken heart. By starting the healing process here, the upward relationship will begin to open and heal.

I was visiting a woman in the hospital who was not responding to physical therapy. Through several visits I learned she was overcome with guilt from a divorce. It affected every part of her life, and of course, all three relationship aspects. Her focus was intensely inward. When she understood that her husband's leaving her for a younger woman was not her fault, the other dimensions of her personal self began to open up, and her progress in physical therapy was almost amazing.

Disenfranchised grief also affects the upward, inward and outward relationships the way a vacuum cleaner distorts the other sounds around it. Finding out what grief issues have not been resolved, especially those that are deep and historic, has a cathartic effect on the whole person and can firmly plant their feet on a spiritual journey that hitherto seemed impossible. The release and expression of love for others, themselves and finally for God allows them to explore their full potential.

Ram Dass, a spiritual teacher, describes helping in a way that captures the essence of the three spirituality aspects (the following parentheticals are mine).

> Service gradually becomes an offering, first to those we are with (outward), but eventually to that greater truth or source of being in which we are all joined in love (upward). Helping becomes an act of reverence, worship, gratitude (upward). It is grace merely to have the chance to serve. Mother Teresa, for example, bending to hold a dying leper, sees there only 'Christ in a distressing disguise'. She's not 'helping a dying leper,' she's loving God (upward), affirming in whomever she's with universal qualities of perfection and beauty . . . as real as this spirit is in us (inward), we have to communicate it to others (outward), in addition to everything else we are doing on their behalf.[211]

---

[211] Ram Dass and Paul Gorman, *How Can I Help? Stories and reflections on service* (New York: Alfred A. Knopt, 1987) , 226.

Our spirituality is all encompassing, inclusive and dynamic, and this spiritual assessment model can be applied to every spiritual discipline, used to explore life's journeys, applied to traditional frameworks, and used as a framework for prayer, mediation, and study.

## THEOLOGICAL REFLECTION AND THEOLOGICAL INSIGHT

Theological reflection is about contemplating something in life in relation to what the bible might have to say about it. I ask, "How does theology speak to me in this situation? Or, "What is God saying to me here?"[212] Some of my patients struggle with great illness and liken it to David battling Goliath. Like David, they want to grow in their trust of the Lord and attack the threatening giant in the power of the Living God.

The old woman sat at one of the card tables in the dining area of the mental health unit weeping and dabbing her eyes. She had two black eyes and a badly scraped nose, and my heart went out to her. I went over and sat down next to her and asked, "How are you doing?" She sniffled and sobbed, "I'm not doing very well." In the course of our conversation, I learned that she had fallen down that morning, landing squarely on her face. And I learned that she was just having trouble coping with life–she was brokenhearted and crushed in spirit. It wasn't long before we were talking politics, religion, family problems, problems with getting old, and laughing occasionally. After forty minutes, I saw that it was time for me to leave. I asked her, "How do you feel?" She looked up smiling, "Much better. Thank you." We hugged, and I left.

---

[212] Patricia O'Connell Killen and John de Beer, *The Art of Theological Reflection*, (New York: Crossroad, 1998), passim.

Theological reflection is the examination of an experience in light of the Bible or Christian tradition, and there are many suggestions on how to do it best. Some people propose a format. With a structure, certain questions prompt a close examination of an experience.

One simple way to do theological reflection, which I use myself, is to contemplate and/or journal on the day's events, conversations, and thoughts by asking a few questions. Although there are many questions we could ask, I would suggest that only two really matter: "Were my actions pleasing to God, and did I love well?" To paraphrase the Apostle Paul, "The only thing that matters is love."[213] Everything else is either not important or has no eternal consequence. A life examined in this light will grow spiritually, and a person who does not want to grow spiritually will not examine their life this way.

Theological insight is different from theological reflection. Insight is received, and reflection is an action. Theological insight is the thought or image that comes, unbidden, when hearing someone share a story, thinking about an event in our lives, or while spending time in prayer and Bible study. The insight come to mind as a thought or picture, often something from the Bible.

Theological insight does not have to happen in a quiet and contemplative environment. In my case, it often happens *in the moment* while visiting patients, when an idea, thought, or image pops into my head that speaks directly and poignantly to the person's issue. Sometimes I have to consider when to speak or even if to speak it. I used to worry that by waiting with the thought, which seemed so appropriate at the time, would vanish forever if it was not shared. But it is seldom appropriate to interrupt the

---

[213] I Cor 13:1-13.

160

story of a person, and I learned not to worry about it so much; that if God allowed, it would come back to mind at the right time. Solomon said it most poetically, "A word aptly spoken is like apples of gold in settings of silver."[214] By growing in the knowledge of the God's Word, the Bible, and committing it to heart; and by reflecting on our lives in the light of God's love and our own expression of it, the Holy Spirit is able to access all of this to bring to the needy the right word at the right time.

## DISENFRANCHISED GRIEF

Dr. Doka published a paper on disenfranchised grief in 1987 and followed it with the highly acclaimed book *Disenfranchised Grief–Hidden Sorrow*. At that time, it was as ground breaking in the area of grief, as Elizabeth Kublar-Ross's book *On Death and Dying* was for death and dying–both impacted the study of thanatology. He hit upon a concept that was not well defined and sought to identify and treat those people who had suffered a loss, but were not afforded the normal opportunities to express their grief and bereavement.

The current book, published in 2002, is divided up into four sections and 26 subject areas (chapters) contributed by leaders in their respected fields. Section 1: Theoretical Overview, in five chapters, takes the reader through the basics of disenfranchised grief and shows how the original concept has been expanded and modified based on research and feedback. Section 2: Clinical Interventions–Tools and Techniques, in four chapters, discusses the role of support groups, group therapy, the role of ritual in treatment, and pastoral counseling. Section 3: Illustrations of Practice, thirteen chapters, are excellent case studies and treatment techniques covering a wide range of

---

[214] Prov 25:11.

situations: Loss of a spouse late in life; grief in the workplace; grief of caregivers; nursing home staff grief over deaths; psychosocial loss and grief; the brokenhearted; loss of an animal companion; losses in child adoption; youth; grief of children; individuals with developmental disabilities; stigmatized death; and culture, class and gender. Section 4: Disenfranchised Grief: Education and Policy, four chapters, discuss politics; classroom education; costs; and Dr. Doka's conclusion.

As you can see, this book will quickly become a reference for the pastoral counselor. In particular, I see it of great value to the hospital or hospice chaplain, because they often meet people struggling with deep, unresolved, grief issues that are disenfranchised or can easily become so.

Disenfranchised grief happens, "when a person experiences a [significant separation or] loss, and the resulting grief is unrecognized by others."[215] The grievers are not accorded the right to grieve because of the circumstances, "the nature of the loss, or the nature of the relationship. So although the person experiences grief, that grief is not openly acknowledged, socially validated, or publicly observed."[216]

The idea of loss implies a detachment of a psychological, physical, and spiritual bond to people, animals, possessions, and property. Our culture teaches us how to mourn: how to behave, think and feel through a loss. There are laws, written and unwritten, and social norms which determine who is allowed to enter a recognized grieving process. For example, in hospice and counseling training, we learn the importance of funerals in facilitating the grieving process and helping people *let go* of their loved one.

---

[215] Doka, *Disenfranchised Grief*, 7.
[216] Doka, *Disenfranchised Grief*, 5.

Grief and the bereavement process become complicated by disenfranchisement and the lack of social support, and it hampers the grief work necessary for healing. If a person is not invited to the funeral, not able to assist with the dying person, shunned, or denied access to the mourning rituals, they carry the pain forward into everything they do and experience–into their lives. Disenfranchisement can bring out intensified emotions, feelings of anger, guilt, powerlessness, and ambivalence, and can all be exasperated by concurrent crises.[217] The chaplain or pastor may see them next, in the midst of a crisis, triggered by something insignificant to us, but actually from the accumulation of unresolved and unrecognized pain.[218] It then becomes the job of the minister to assist and help the person find healing. The closure of these old wounds can be bring healing on many levels.

Sometimes the different meanings of words can be confusing. This section on definitions might be helpful:

> Bereavement is a loss; grief is the response to that loss. Grief work is the work that must be accomplished in order to move through the pain associated with the loss. Mourning consists of social expectations as well as cultural definitions and rules that tell us how important our loss is; whether we have the right to grieve; and, if so, how much, how long, and in what ways we can and should do so.[219]

It is also important here to note that while Doka was the editor and authored several chapters, other contributors tried to define these terms their own way. For example: In Chapter 3, "Revisiting the Concept of Disenfranchised Grief," Charles A. Corr pointed out that "Grief reactions are not the whole of the human response to loss.[220]

---

[217] Charles A. Carr, "Revisiting the Concept of Disenfranchised Grief," in *Disenfranchised Grief: New directions, challenges, and strategies for practice* (ed. Kenneth J. Doka, Champaign, Ill.: Research Press, 2002), 41-42.
[218] Howard W. Stone, *Crisis Counseling* (Minneapolis: Fortress Press, 1993), 23-4.
[219] Carr, "Revisiting the Concept," in *Disenfranchised Grief* (ed. Doka), 30.
[220] Carr, "Revisiting the Concept," in *Disenfranchised Grief* (ed. Doka), 49.

He meant that the grief component involves feelings and emotions, but there are other aspects of the grief: somatic and behavioral. People may allow a feelings-oriented grief, but disenfranchise the griever if they have somatic or behavioral responses also. There is more on this aspect in the discussion to follow: The ways individuals grieve.

In Doka's first book, he identified three groups of disenfranchised grief: (1) Lack of recognition of the relationship, (2) Lack of acknowledgment of the loss, and (3) Exclusion of the griever. If a person is not allowed to attend the funeral for one of these three reasons, their grief work is hindered or disenfranchised. So the funeral ritual, a critical event in most cultures, gives structure and accepted expression.

Now Doka has added two more disenfranchised grief categories: (4) Circumstances of the death, and (5) The ways individuals grieve.[221]

As I review each of the five categories of disenfranchised grief, examples will come to your mind.


### LACK OF RECOGNITION OF THE RELATIONSHIP

Close familial relationships, spouses and kin, are legitimized and recognized by cultures, churches, businesses and governments. A close and enduring friendship, *being closer than a brother,* does not ensure time off from work to attend the funeral. If you are a member of the military, you can attend the funeral of a grandparent, only if you can prove they raised you. "Lovers, friends, neighbors, foster parents, colleagues, in-laws, stepparents, stepchildren, caregivers, counselors, coworkers, and roommates may have

---

[221] Doka, *Disenfranchised Grief*, 1.

long lasting and intensely interactive relationships," but find they are unable to express their grief or get it recognized publicly.[222]

Internet-based relationships, although often hampered by distance and truthful vagueness, are nevertheless sources of deep feeling communication and shared intimacy. In one sense it is impersonal, yet as feelings and dreams are shared, a true intimacy develops. The popular movie *You've Got Mail* showed how Internet-based relationships and intimacies cause grief when the email is not answered or they end suddenly and without explanation. When Meg Ryan said she had developed a deep, yet unusual relationship with a man, Tom Hanks guessed that it was on the Internet and said gravely, "Those are very powerful words, 'You've got mail.' "

The loss of past relationships can cause present grief. I have known divorced women who grieved when the former spouse, sometimes many years later, decided to marry someone else. It brought finality to the earlier loss and ended any hope, whether rational or not, of reconciliation. How does the boss or society react when they learn that this person is staying home from work mourning a marriage that officially ended sixteen years earlier?

### LOSS IS NOT ACKNOWLEDGED

The *loss is not acknowledged* category comes in two parts: (1) Think of this as the loss of dreams: the loss of an imagined future, and (2) secondary losses.

Loss of an imagined future. In a society where abortion is routine and more prevalent than at any other time in world history, a woman mourning the loss of the unborn child is seldom supported or acknowledged. Miscarriages, early stillborn children,

---

[222] Doka, *Disenfranchised Grief*, 10.

children put up for adoption, the loss of a dear pet, all produce a deep sense of loss for people, but society as a whole might wonder what all the fuss is about.

In another case, people may suffer from loss when the person they are grieving for is still alive and in a coma, perhaps medically brain dead, or have a changed personality due to mental illness, addiction, or addiction recovery. An example from this book talked about how a woman mourned the loss of her husband's ability to speak and communicate with her as his ALS progressed, more than his death that followed. The same would be true of hospice caregivers, who tend to the needs of their loved ones 24/7 and watch them slowly fade. Who they were as people is no longer the person lying in the bed.

There is loss and grief when a person's sense of identity is taken away. The loss of a job or a career has been known to drive some men into deep depression. The movie *Falling Down* with Michael Douglas, showed how a job loss could bring about profound grief, anger and despair. His job loss grief was further exasperated by compounding crises as he tried to get home from work, and his coping skills were challenged at multiple levels.

Secondary losses. Transitions set people up for loss, and most people have had secondary losses. Life is about transitions, and usually we learn to cope with these transitions and the challenges they present. A person graduates from high school, but leaves friends and family behind to go to college. A person doesn't get good grades and has to postpone or change career plans. They break a leg and can't compete in a race they've dreamed of all their life. We can think of many examples, and probably many we have experienced ourselves.

## GRIEVER IS EXCLUDED

I experienced this form of disenfranchisement when I was five years old and my brother, Timothy, who was three, died of leukemia. Young children were not expected to have grieving issues. My father told me Tim died, and then I was left alone, as far as I can remember. My parents and teachers thought I was a real problem when my behavior changed, and I did poorly in school. No one made the connection, but I did many years later.

Very old mentally ill people who show little emotion, and people stigmatized by the circumstances of death (AIDS, drugs, suicide, murder), are often excluded from the usual social grief processes. In the hospital where I worked as a chaplain, I found that the very old are often treated as children, much to their consternation. Their inability to fend for themselves, and their need for basic assistance, puts them at a disadvantage in a robust, mobile, self-assured, and self-centered society. Our society expects to put the embarrassing or unusual people and circumstances behind them and move on to more culturally normative experiences. There are probably many books just on these issues.

## CIRCUMSTANCES OF THE DEATH

As mentioned above, the circumstances causing grief can disenfranchise people. People can be stigmatized by society if their loved one died of AIDS, alcohol, or drugs, committed murder and was executed, was the victim of murder or suicide, died a prostitute, and many other things. Other family members, friends, and society show some kind of disapproval or nonrecognition, which then brings out feelings of discomfort, embarrassment, anger, shame, confusion, denial, guilt, and perhaps anxiety.

167

In the hospital, it was not uncommon for family members to acknowledge the final wishes of the patient who desired no extraordinary lifesaving efforts (i.e. the DNR– "Do Not Resuscitate" order in the medical records), and then feel guilty and disenfranchised by the death. The death of a loved one puts the family in crisis, even when expected. The term *crisis,* by definition, places them in a vulnerable and suggestive state.[223] It is important, as a chaplain, to recognize this opportunity to ensure that the family grieves properly and does not blame themselves or suffer from unnecessary guilt or anger. I've done this by educating them as soon as possible–often at the bedside, and also through family prayer; where I lead them in committing the loved one into God's hands. In one case, where a young man had died suddenly and unexpectedly, all I had to say was, "To be absent from the body…", and I paused. Then the family members, from a local Baptist church, gathered around the body lying on the hospital bed all said together, "Is to be present with the Lord." I knew they had set foot on the path to acknowledging the death and grieving appropriately.

## WAYS INDIVIDUALS GRIEVE

In western culture, at the beginning of the bereavement, people are allowed to grieve loudly–wailing, crying, falling on the floor and whatever. Very quickly, though, this becomes unacceptable, and if it continues beyond that *unwritten* point in time, the grieving person may get a sedative. People who grieve deeply but quietly, showing little if any emotion, might be seen as just as odd, but they do not alarm people around them.

---

[223] Howard Clinebell, *Basic Types of Pastoral Care and Counseling–Resources for the ministry of healing and growth* (Nashville: Abingdon, 1984), 183.

As a hospital chaplain, it is important to know how different cultures and religions express their grief to ensure hospital staff (emergency room, ICU) are not unduly alarmed, or so that the hospital staff can be warned ahead of time.

A Samoan mother lost her firstborn son in a motorcycle accident. She became hysterical when she learned he had also been hit by a truck. One staff member, in great alarm, suggested she be given a sedative. I assured him that she needed to grieve deeply and loudly for a time, and that the hysteria would pass. To everyone's relief, including my own, after five minutes it did.

If the person has grieved the significant loss, attended the funeral and *gotten on with life,* their coworkers will not tolerate too much moping around after a while. They will get tired of making excuses for the perceived poor behavior and encourage the griever to, "Get over it," or, "My God man, it was just a dog!" or, "Just accept God's will." or, "Go home and eat a good meal and get a good night's sleep, and you'll be 'right as rain' tomorrow . . ." or words to that effect.

"Just accept God's will." Disenfranchised grief has pastoral components which I ran into on a weekly basis working in a hospital and at hospice. It might also be a good subject for educating a congregation from the pulpit. That sermon might include what to say to a grieving person, different aspects of grief as discussed here, and how to act and help as those people struggle through their grief work.

As a chaplain, we desire to bring or facilitate healing. We want to encourage the disenfranchised griever to grieve without society's permission. We want to help them recognize what happened, why, and then what they can do about it. Coming alongside them, exploring coping skills and mechanisms, and appropriate expressions and opportunities, will promote healing and start them on the road to closure. Every person is unique and requires a unique approach. If we listen carefully, they will help us help them.

## SELF-CARE, SOUL-CARE

Self-care comes in four parts: physical, mental, relational, and spiritual. I left out emotional because I feel that it flows through all of the parts. Caring for each piece takes a little work, but the long-term benefits are worth it. There is a saying around exercise circles: *use it or loose it*. The following lists will give you a few ideas on things you can do to *exercise* self-care in your life, and some of these, of course, will fit into more than one category. Is fishing a physical past time or a spiritual past time? Might depend on the size of the fish and where you are fishing. If you go fishing with friends and loved ones, does it become a relational and mental refreshment also? I've listed many things in each category, but many more will come to your mind as you read them. Personally, my own self-care comes out of all categories all the time and is easily mixed up and blended, and I greatly value spontaneity. George McDonald wrote something that I have on my wall, which I apply to my own self-care, "The blessedness of life depends more upon its interests than upon its comforts."[224] I've tested this saying and have found it to be true, and now it's a part of my life.

Physical activity refreshes the body and the mind. Eating food good for us, taking vitamins, pacing ourselves, giving and receiving hugs, maintaining our weight, limiting alcohol consumption, dancing, exercising, walking, hiking, taking your camera out into

---

[224] George McDonald, "Chapter XX: Robert Falconer," *Classic Reader Web.* http://classicreader.com/read.php/sid.1/bookid.1171/sec.58/ (11 Nov 2006).

nature, wearing a seatbelt in the car, not smoking, bathing regularly, and getting enough sleep all promote our physical self-care.

Mental self-care is managed by laughing and playing whenever possible, staying curious about life, continuing to learn, good affirmative self-talk, reading books and listening to music, saving money for spending, maintaining a clean environment, facing and resolving old conflicts, and keeping time in our schedule for ourselves.

Relational self-care means we live in and have healthy relationships with others and ourselves. We seek help when we need it, have friends and mentors to talk to, help in community, read to children, play with children, go bowling, go dancing, go to dinner with friends and family, nurture loving sex, spend time with people we love, accept their comments about us, when necessary defend others, and treat ourselves right. The relation and spiritual aspects easily overlap, because spirituality is about how we relate to a higher power, ourselves, and community.

Spiritual self-care is about disciplines, attitudes, and beliefs. There are many disciplines and many more books on what the disciplines are and how to practice them. The spiritual disciplines that nourish our spirit are prayer, giving and receiving love, meditation, fasting, giving money away, faith, just stopping, cultivate rituals that refresh, honoring the Sabbath, meeting for worship, knowing and keeping our purpose in life, nurturing our relationships, spending time in quiet places and nature, listening to sacred and soothing music, spending quality time with family and children, reading inspirational books, playing instruments, playing with children and pets, and helping others.

The spiritual is also about attitudes that speak to us: gratitude, thankfulness, compassion, respect, humility, long-suffering, patience, kindness, forgiving others and letting them forgive us, being content with what we have, and not harboring bitterness or anger. It is no surprise that the Apostle Paul called some of these the fruit of the Spirit, because they are the results of spiritual care.[225]

Our beliefs are informed by our culture, our family, and our personal journey. What we believe can have a very powerful influence on our spiritual understanding of our place in the world and eternity. It is also about our dreams, hopes, and loves. In this area, deep feelings of contentment and disturbance, calmness and restlessness, can flow through eddies and currents as we struggle with our faith or settle into our beliefs. Self-care in this area can be nourished from all of the others and just as easily overlooked. If we say that we know what we believe and that's that, then it seems to limit what God might want to speak to us about. If we can't hear what God is saying to us, our spiritual self-care will suffer.

Spiritual disciplines are a major aspect of self-care and leadership development. The leader that only uses *Best Business Practices*, *Management by Objectives*, and techniques like *Six Sigma* management principles, can take stock holders and church ministries to undreamed of heights, and yet be completely bankrupt inside themselves. It is essential for all leaders, not just the spiritual and religious, to make time for spiritual development and disciplines in their lives in order to be successful, holistically, as people.

Our brain handles stress differently, depending on how it is used. If we feel emotionally worn out and a little depressed, the right hemisphere of emotion, creativity, and well-being is overused. To counterbalance, do something that uses the left side of the brain, which is more concrete and matter-of-fact. Activities like math, writing poetry,

---

[225] Gal 5:22.

reading something technical or philosophical, learn a language or instrument, and organizing something calms down the emotional side. Occasionally, when my hospice and hospital chaplain work wring me out emotionally, I go home and do some sudoku number puzzles: I've gotten pretty good at them.

Likewise, if the left side of the brain is overtaxed and burdened with the stresses of time, schedules, tasks, and studies, switch to the creative right side. In these cases, I paint, play an instrument, play a game, go kayaking, read something fun, or watch a favorite old movie.

Our attitude toward life has a lot to do with our care of self. The 90/10 rule says that ten percent of life is what happens to you, and ninety percent is how we react. If we keep this in mind, the various aspects of self-care-the physical, mental, relational, and spiritual-are much easier to manage, requiring less purposeful work. Father Alfred D'Souza wrote *happiness is a journey, not a destination,*[226] but the saying has been added to and expanded over the years, as people try to say a little more about how we take that journey: *Happiness is a journey, not a destination, so work like you don't need the money, sing like you're in the shower, love like you've never been hurt before, dance like no one's watching, and live as if heaven is on earth.*

---

[226] Alfred D'Souza, "Happiness is a Journey," *Fleurdelis Web.*
http://www.fleurdelis.com/happinessisajourney.htm (11 Nov 2006).

"They will speak of the glorious splendor of your majesty, and I will meditate on your wonderful works."[227]

Is this you? When you try to sit quietly, in a short time your thoughts are all over the place, your mind is continually grasping. It seems that the harder you try to sit quietly the more your mind races from one thought to the next, wondering if something is done, or how that will happen, who will do what, what you'll say at the talk, what you'll write in the note, what's on the schedule for today, who's in the hospital, is my phone on, and a million other things. In this state of mind, you may go to bed and not be able to get to sleep, or you may wake up in the middle of the night and not be able to get back to sleep. You may be working on a simple task during the day, and the thought about something completely different will intrude, and you won't be able to finish, or you'll get sidetracked. You might want to spend some quiet time in prayer or reading and your thoughts betray you-sometimes thoughts that do not even seem like they belong to you.

The purpose of true meditation is to have a single thought. This cannot be done unless the mind is cleared of its racing thoughts. With a little practice, clearing the mind is easy, and the rambling and jumbled thoughts will fall away, powerless.

The following technique is very old and has been used for thousands of years to calm the soul. It has nothing to do with religion or spirituality, but has everything to do with mental health. At the beginning you will need a quiet place, but with just a little practice, you will be able to calm your soul while driving the car, sitting on an airplane, working in the yard, waiting in line, or exercising-literally, anywhere and anytime.

---

[227] Psalm 145:5.

First, find a quiet place, sit down, and breathe. Breathe slowly and deeply and listen to your breathing. After a minute, start to count. Breathe in deeply, then exhale and think *one*. Breath in slowly, then exhale slowly and think *two*. Breathe in, then exhale and think *three*. Breathe in, then exhale and think *four*. Then repeat with one and go to four again, and again. No less than four, and no more than four. If a stray thought comes into your mind, acknowledge it, *I see you*, but continue to breathe and count. Keep your focus stays on the breathing and the numbers. You do not need an image of the numbers, just the thought. It takes anywhere from a few hours to a few days to really get the hang of this. You can master it, if you practice every day, in a week or two.[228]

In this way, I pray myself into a quiet place, where foreign, evil, and racing thoughts cannot intrude. It becomes a special place, a private retreat, where I can feel nurtured and refreshed, with a sense of healing. In this place, I open my bible and read, pray, sing songs to the Lord, play my flute or guitar, read an inspirational book, even write a letter to someone, or just sit quietly-listening.

In time you will be able to substitute the numbers with a word or phrase. But for now, keep it simple. If in the future you are using a word or phrase and the racing thoughts seem to intrude, acknowledge the thought, then go back to breathing the numbers. This is basic meditation, and it always works. There have been occasions when the stresses of life caused me to go all the way back to the breathing numbers routine in order to calm down inside: back to the basics. I did not see this as failure or a detour; but rather, I saw it as a blessed option.

---

[228] Paul Wilson, *The Calm Technique: Meditation without magic or mysticism*, (New York: Barnes & Noble Books, 1985), passim.

By itself, the breathing numbers is a quieting exercise, but when it is applied to other spiritual disciplines, it broadens and deepens those areas; for example, speaking and listening in prayer. One time Jesus and the disciples were in the temple watching the people pray, and Jesus saw an opportunity to teach.

> The Pharisee stood up and prayed about himself: "God, I thank you that I am not like other men-robbers, evildoers, adulterers-or even like this tax collector. I fast twice a week and give a tenth of all I get." But the tax collector stood at a distance. He would not even look up to heaven, but beat his breast and said, "*God, have mercy on me, a sinner.*" I tell you that this man, rather than the other, went home justified before God. For everyone who exalts himself will be humbled, and he who humbles himself will be exalted.[229]

When our minds are cleared, we feel more centered, and when our minds are cleared, it is then that we can hear God speak more clearly to us. When you have mastered the breathing numbers, substitute them with the phrase, *God, have mercy on me, a sinner*. This is known in the Eastern Orthodox church as the *Jesus Prayer*. It is the most simple and powerful of prayers, because it speaks of who God is to us, our hope for the future, and our humility and dependence before God. When I breathe prayers, I do it in four breaths. On the inward breath, I think *Oh*, and on the outward *God*; on the inward, I think *have*, and on the outward *mercy*: *Oh God, have mercy, on me, a sinner*; or, *Oh Jesus, have mercy, on Joel, a sinner*.

I also pray about spiritual renewal and transformation. In several places, the scriptures tell us to be transformed in our hearts and minds, but it is obvious that it is not in our power to do the transforming: It is the work of the Holy Spirit.[230] By presenting myself to God and inviting the Spirit to make that transformation, it happens. It's like watching grass grow, it can be so slow, but it does happen. In this quiet place, with my

---

[229] Luke 18:11-14.
[230] Rom 12:1-2, Eph 4:23, Psalm 26:2.

mind cleared of all other thoughts, I breathe: *Oh Lord, I present myself, transform my heart and mind, into your image.*

I also pray for the Lord to reveal my hidden faults; those things that I am not aware of. In the Psalms, David wrote, "Forgive my hidden faults. Keep your servant also from willful sins; may they not rule over me."[231] Because of this prayer, the Spirit has revealed things to me, about me, that I was not even aware of. Hidden faults and willful sins can destroy religious leaders, as we've seen in the news. If the Spirit reveals them to us, it also helps heal those areas of our lives, which we give up for transformation and renewal.

Restoration of the soul comes through mediation and times of quiet. "He maketh me to lie down in green pastures: he leadeth me beside the still waters. He restoreth my soul."[232]

> Laurie decided to pray. She prayed quietly, without words, meditating on a single, unspoken question suspended in the silence. As she prayed, she listened. She let the worries of her whole life fall away and listened to this singular question; every beat of her heart became a prayer. . . . Only at rest can we hear what we have not heard before, and be led to what is most deeply beautiful, necessary, and true.[233]

"Morning by morning, O Lord, you hear my voice; morning by morning I lay my requests before you and wait in expectation."[234] How can we wait, if our spirit is restless, and we cannot be silent in our minds?

I am not saying we will not wrestle with our thoughts and decisions. But when we want to take a break from these mental pursuits and gymnastics, then there is a place to go. It is the act of stopping that is most important. This begins the process of setting

---

[231] Psalm 19:13.
[232] Psalm 23:2-3a, *KJV*.
[233] Wayne Muller, *Sabbath: Finding rest, renewal, and delight in our busy lives* (New York: Bantam, 1999), 162.
[234] Psalm 5:3.

boundaries around your inner self and outer self; a spiritual space that says, "This space is sacred." Honoring this part of you helps develop emotional and spiritual maturity: It is quality time well invested.

I boldly suggest that of all the self-care things you can do for yourself, meditation may be the most valuable and most rewarding, because it allows you to enter into and experience a sense of spiritual tranquility.

## SUFFERANCE SELF-CARE

Life often brings suffering. In almost every life, there is a time when the suffering cannot be avoided, but must rather be gone through, experienced, and absorbed. The reasons for this are many, although we may not know why we experience something in the moment. In my own case, I've discovered the meaning of some suffering many years later, and at other times right when it was happening.

Sufferance self-care means the care of self that comes from patient endurance through great pain, sorrow, distress, or misfortune.[235] It is during those times in our lives, when we retreat to desert places and lonely places. Whether out of spiritual conviction or to lick our wounds, we find ourselves practically or completely alone with our feelings.

Like Moses, I've retreated to different desert places to recover and grow closer to God. A good example is the periodic attack of arthritis that affects my feet, neck, and back. During these times, I've get little or no relief through massage, medicine, or anything, and I've carried this image in my mind and heart of clinging to the legs of

---

[235] Dictionary.com, "Sufferance," (Based on the American Heritage Dictionary of the English Language, 4 ed.), http://dictionary.reference.com/browse/sufferance (11 Nov 2006).

Jesus, sometimes almost desperately, assuring him that he is not going anywhere without me.

> After this there was a feast of the Jews; and Jesus went up to Jerusalem. Now there is at Jerusalem by the sheep market a pool, which is called in the Hebrew tongue Bethesda, having five porches. In these lay a great multitude of impotent folk, of blind, halt, withered, waiting for the moving of the water. For an angel went down at a certain season into the pool, and troubled the water: whosoever then first after the troubling of the water stepped in was made whole of whatever disease he had.[236]

It reminds me of the story about the physician at the Pool of Bethesda, as related by Ken Gire in *The North Face of God*. The angel comes at certain times to trouble the water, which brings healing to the first person to jump in. Late one night, a physician comes to the pool seeking healing for his afflictions. The angel appears to him and tells him that healing is not for him. He leans toward the pool and pleads, explaining that if healed he can do so much more.

> The angel stands a moment in silence, as if picking his words carefully. "Without your wound where would your power be?" he asks at last. "It is your very remorse that makes your low voice tremble into the hearts of men. The very angels themselves cannot persuade the wretched and blundering children on earth as can one human being broken on the wheels of living. In Love's service, only the wounded soldiers can serve. Draw back."[237]

We go to the desert or are called to the desert to learn something we cannot learn anywhere else. Speaking of this desert experience as a necessary ingredient of leadership, Henry Nouwen wrote:

> Who can save a child from a burning house without taking the risk of being hurt by the flames? Who can listen to a story of loneliness and despair without taking the risk of experiencing similar pains in his own heart and even losing his precious piece of mind? In short: "Who can take away suffering without entering

---

[236] John 5:1-4, *KJV*.
[237] Ken Gire, *The North Face of God* (Colorado Springs: Alive Communications, 2005), 108-9.

it?" The great illusion of leadership is to think that man can be led out of the desert by someone who has never been there.[238]

## SPIRITUALITY OF SELF-CARE

I have defined spirituality as *upward, inward, and outward aspects of a relationship and connection to something "other" than our selves.* Tying these three aspects together into the journey metaphor, gives us another view of how to care for ourselves. That's the point, that life is a journey, life is a pilgrimage, life is more than the start point and the destination. It's about what you do in the middle, and how your life is lived in the middle.

The idea of life being a pilgrimage comes out of the Bible, with the sense that it is not this present life but the next we are living for: It is a spiritual pilgrimage. Jesus explained this in Luke 18, "I tell you the truth," Jesus said to them, "no one who has left home or wife or brothers or parents or children for the sake of the kingdom of God will fail to receive many times as much in this age and, in the age to come, eternal life." In the Psalms we read, "You have made known to me the path of life; you will fill me with joy in your presence, with eternal pleasures at your right hand." [239] And in the poetic Psalm 42, "As the hart panteth after the water brooks, so panteth my soul after thee, O God. My soul thirsteth for God, for the living God: when shall I come and appear before God?" [240]

Doris Connelly wrote elegantly about the pilgrim in relation to a tourist visiting a holy site.[241] But I want to look at the pilgrim in relation to the attitudes people have in traveling through this life, in general. The main difference between a pilgrim and a traveler is attitude. The traveler is more concerned about the destination; it is their

---

[238] Nouwen, *The Wounded Healer*, 72.
[239] Psalm 16:11.
[240] Psalm 42:1, *KJV*.
[241] Doris Donnelly, "Pilgrims and Tourists: Conflicting metaphors for the Christian journey to God," Spring 1992. *Spirituality Today Web.* http://www.spiritualitytoday.org/spir2day/924411donnelly.html (18 Nov 2006).

primary goal, and how far and how fast they go. Some people live their lives as travelers, driving furiously to get as many miles in during the day as their physical strength can muster. They accumulate things and experiences because they believe their happiness depends on these things.

For pilgrims, the destination is also important as well as the ultimate goal; but in the here and now-the moment, the journey itself is more important. In the journey, Pilgrims are transformed by their purposeful attention, interaction, and commitment to the world around them, because life is about our relationships-with our God (upward), transformation and insight (inward), and loving, helping, and nurturing friends and community (outward). Instead of skipping over the surface of life like a flat stone, the Pilgrim plunges into the water and settles into the depths of life. In this way, the Pilgrim finds true contentment.

Many people believe that the purpose of life is to acquire things until they die, but more does not make life better; it just means you have more stuff. Life is not even about the accumulation of experiences, although theme parks and advertising agencies will try to convince people otherwise. The Mennonites get it: living more with less. Life is about quality, not quantity. Is there a secret to finding happiness in simplicity or in the quality of life lived?

In the book, *Tuesday's with Morrie,* Morrie is dying of ALS (Lou Gehrig's disease), and Mitch is always amazed at Morrie's great attitude as his health declines in the face of certain death. Mitch asked Morrie, that if he was perfectly healthy for twenty-four hours, what would he do. When Morrie described his perfect 24-hour day, it was very ordinary: simple, average. He would have a simple breakfast, go swimming, have different groups of friends over for lunch, go for a walk in nature, go to a restaurant in the evening, then go dancing until exhausted. Finally, he would go home for a deep, wonderful sleep. Mitch finally realized that the whole point of the perfect day for Morrie was that it was completely simple and average. That it was about simple pleasures, doing things he loved, and being with the people he loved.

How does a person discover their own spirituality and become a Pilgrim? Discovering your spirituality is often portrayed as something almost mystical, elusive, and out there. Like you have to eat tofu and do yoga and sit in funny positions, or do funny exercises, or smell exotic smells, touch crystals, or listen to flute music in order to find or capture a sense of the spiritual. Yet, to pause and watch the fly by of a honking flight of Canadian geese does something to us: Our soul is stirred. Beauty stirs us: To stand in the doorway of the house one morning, pausing with the coffee cup in one hand, to watch the blazing, iridescent, streaming rainbow of colors on the clouds, as the sun seeps over the eastern horizon. Quiet stirs us: To lean back in your chair, closing your eyes, and listening to your breathing – in and out, slowly, in a natural rhythm.

Like all journeys, the pilgrimage life starts with a first step, but it is not a quest or a mission to find something. You literally don't need to go anywhere. Your spirituality is nurtured in the life around you, the life you live; like the tendrils of smoke rising from the yet flameless twigs and grass, gently blown, even whispered into creation. To pause, to consider, or to think about your experience in the moment or a relationship and what they mean to you and what you mean to others. Only letting that moment of reflection speak to your soul; albeit, you might barely, perhaps at first only subconsciously, know the language. But you were made to hear and speak this language. You were made to walk in the Garden in the cool of the evening with your Creator. You were made to notice that you feel something different, special, peaceful, and in time to notice and feel that it touches something deep down inside. And in that touching, you feel refreshed; you experience a calm, a peacefulness, even a sense of gentleness. A voice only you can hear deep inside, not in your head, but in your heart of hearts whispers, "Linger here."

Here you are, in the moment, reading these lines. What would happen if you stopped, let your hands fall to your lap and became quiet? Does it help to close your eyes? Does it help to listen to your breathing? Don't ask any questions, just take it in. Let it be, and watch, listen, and soak it up.

Some people reading this will write it off as so much mumbo jumbo and contemplative mysticism. But if you are really doing that, more than anyone else you need to embrace this Pilgrim Spirituality. Ask yourself why you have rejected this idea of spirituality and internal growth, knowing yourself, benefiting others, and living simply. Does the Pilgrim journey not fit your lifestyle, or does your lifestyle not fit the journey?

## RETREATS – A TIME OF HEALING

Recently someone asked me, "How will there be healing at a retreat?" This is a good question, and it is actually asking many different things, one of which is, "What is a retreat?"

The idea behind any retreat is to holistically seek to bring heart, mind, body and spirit into renewal. Retreats can take many forms, but just being offered a retreat by the agency tells the person that their well-being is valued, that they are respected for what they do, and that they might be under some extraordinary stresses. In a sense, the healing starts right there – with the invitation. When people are told they are going to have a retreat, they sigh with relief and are thankful. At first they don't even ask where it will be, how much time will be allotted for it, or what the theme might be. They are just thankful that it is happening.

Healing also takes place on a retreat if it can be in a pleasant and natural environment, like in the woods, near the ocean, or some other quiet sanctuary outside the busy-ness and time-bound world we live in. The cell phones and pagers are turned off, quiet soothing music is played, and a time of decompression takes place. Sometimes it is called *getting centered*, where the cares of the world and work give place to something different. That something different is often completely different from what everyone experiences on a daily basis: calmness. And in entering into this sense of calm, there is safety, freedom, and peace; again, all elements of healing. Before a retreat has even officially started, healing has started with this change in environment.

Many retreats have an educational element. Some people like to speak about the nature of losses, grief, and how we cope. Some like to speak on the value of meditation, quiet times, giving, writing, poems, story telling, reconciliation, work, and many other things. Some retreats are silent, and other retreats offer personal care support, like massages.

Retreats are about spirituality, and another question that might be asked is, "How do losses affect us spiritually?" All of life has a spiritual element to it, and this is often addressed during a retreat. The losses we experience impact us on many levels, and the retreat might be the only time that some people can look at the losses in different ways and from different perspectives.

What is spirituality? What is it about some losses that affect us down deep inside? How has our previous experience with loss informed our new experience? Do we grow or close up? What can we do? The answers to these questions are different for each of us, but the answers, and discovering for ourselves what these are about, bring healing.

Taking all of these together and bringing them together into an activity is another way we find healing. Some retreats do something in the garden or with nature – digging in the earth, planting things, walking, singing, meditating. Some do something in music or the arts–listening to soothing music, playing instruments or someone playing contemplatively, drawing, having the retreat at an art gallery. And many retreats are about meditation, contemplation, and prayer.

One example of finding healing in artistic expression is through finger painting. Finger painting is fun, primitive, often takes us back to our childhood, is something we all can do, and is something we can do individually and as a group. Large sheets of watercolor paper and jars of paint can be purchased at a local art supply store. A short period of instruction is followed by the free expression of painting and learning what the possibilities are in this art form. As people become familiar with the medium, they can paint their own picture at the top of a one-page calendar on watercolor paper, which they can take home and proudly show friends and family. Finally, everyone comes together to create a commemorative poster of the retreat, making a giant flower out of hand prints in different colors, and pictures of everyone at the retreat fill the center. This poster could be prominently displayed in the office the next day, carrying that healing energy back into the workplace.

## CHAPTER 8 – CONCLUSION

## PROBLEM RESTATED

Traditionally, chaplains don't tend to draw attention to themselves as they quietly go about their business. But the needs of people are growing and society is changing. I say *the needs of people are growing* because of the growing gap between the have's and the have not's, more people outside the church than in (many unchurched or dechurched), a growing discontent and violence in the world evidenced by school shootings and terrorism, generalized fears and angers, and the many people who seem to have a spiritual thirst for something they can't even identify.

In chaplaincy and in many churches, leadership, management, and ministry have a synergistic effect when they come together in response to a problem or crisis. An understanding of chaplaincy dynamics, scope, methods, possibilities, and issues in relation to this effect is vital to this growing field in four areas: (1) It helps prepare people for ministry as chaplains, whether clergy or lay; (2) It benefits those already in chaplaincy ministry; (3) It helps clergy reexamine their ministry to determine if they are where God wants them; and, (4) It serves to teach everyone, including upper-level management and senior church leaders (first-chair leaders), of the roles, actual or potential, that chaplains can fill in response to the growing needs of people.

If chaplaincy is to be effective across a broad spectrum of ministry and in the great diversity of settings, it is important to standardize training overall, and if appropriate, train chaplains in the area of management. This will be a giant step in this growing field and increase the professionalism of the group as a whole. Success in ministry and the quality of ministry do not happen by accident; they are the purposeful result of a response to a divine calling, coupled with sincere effort, effective training, respect for people, and skillful execution.

## IMPORTANCE OF THE PROBLEM RESTATED

Chaplains are leaders, and they must be at the forefront of ministry to people on the fringes of our churches and society. Without chaplains helping to meet the growing needs of these people, we will not be fulfilling the mandate to take the Gospel into the whole world, addressing the justice needs of people, or helping alleviate suffering. Simply put, we might finally reach the unreached peoples groups of foreign countries and fail in our mission to reach the people at home.

Chaplain leadership can be enigmatic. The leadership dynamics and concepts in the ministry of chaplains flow from different sources and perspectives, then are articulated in a variety of ways which do not necessarily fit with the standard literature on leadership. Yet, leadership concepts applicable to chaplains can be found in all leadership studies, in their various forms and possibilities. Chaplains are ministers and leaders outside the traditional church building to people who need clergy support, and they often exert great influence on the people they encounter. Although some chaplaincy organizations have continued to challenge their members to grow in training and professionalism, this is not true everywhere. In many areas, people are answering the call to chaplaincy, but are having to learn on the job, through trial and error, and their effectiveness, success, and quality are very elusive or spotty at best. This study addresses some of the areas necessary for successful chaplaincy, although each ministry is unique and has its own challenges.

In this study I want to look at the history of chaplains and the associated leadership perspectives; look briefly at different types of chaplaincies; discuss contemporary church leadership, chaplain management and leadership dynamics; then look at the work of chaplains, some of their tools, and associated leadership issues.

## CONCLUDING THOUGHTS

Although there are many wonderful stories about how people were positively ministered to by chaplains, they don't tend to draw attention to themselves as they go quietly about their business. But as we move into the post-modern world of the 21st century, the needs of people are growing and society is changing. I say this because of the growing gap between the "have's" and the "have not's," more people outside the church than in (many unchurched or dechurched), a growing discontent and violence in the world evidenced by school shootings, terrorism, and generalized fears and angers, and the many people who seem to have a spiritual thirst for something they can't even identify. I believe there is more of a need for chaplains now than ever before.

Chaplains are leaders, and they must be at the forefront of ministry on the fringes of our churches and society. Without chaplains helping to meet the growing needs of these people, our neighbors, we will not succeed. We will not fulfill the mandate of Christ to take the Gospel into all the world, we will not meet people where they need help the most, and we will turn a blind eye to the suffering around us. Simply put, we might finally reach the unreached peoples groups of foreign countries and fail in our mission to reach the people at home, our neighbors lying on the side of society's proverbial road.

The history of chaplaincy taught us that chaplains have a long and storied ministry to people in great need. Chaplains have been at the point of people's needs and suffering, even at the cost of their lives. They led with pastoral authority and with authority delegated by people, and when they saw a need, they worked to fill it.

The leadership and management abilities of chaplains has not always been well understood, but chaplains are definitely leaders, getting their authority and power from a divine source and from people, groups, and agencies. Most chaplains work in a specific area of ministry to a specific group of people. In these positions, their skills are often specialized and can be developed further with training. If chaplains desire a management position or find themselves in one, they can develop those skills necessary for success.

Chaplains are professionals. Whether serving in a hospital or a truck stop, a police station or an airport, it is important to address the particular needs of the people and grow through experience and training in order to lead and minister better.

Chaplain training is often targeted to specific ministries. For example, Clinical Pastoral Education (CPE), as the name implies, is usually for people going into healthcare chaplaincies, although many seminaries require at least one quarter of CPE in order to familiarize students with the needs of patients. Some seminaries are teaching chaplain courses, but it is not widespread. Chaplain training could be improved if all seminaries recognized the need for chaplain training and offered basic and advanced courses. Appendix C offers an outline for an *Introduction to Chaplaincy* course, and a variety of supplementary courses.

With increased knowledge of chaplain contributions to society and more specific chaplain training, society will benefit in ways we can scarcely imagine. A person is going to read this and think of a new place for chaplaincy that meets the peculiar and particular needs of a new group of people. Who knows, in ten or twenty years, maybe there will be more seminarians training to be chaplains than traditional clergy and more chaplaincies than churches.

# APPENDIX A – CHAPLAIN ORGANIZATIONS AND LINKS

## DISCLAIMER

Internet websites and webpages can be dropped (link broken) at almost any time, either intentionally or by accident, so I cannot guarantee that they will be visible if you use the links I provided below to find them.

## BROKEN LINKS

I would suggest that if a link is broken, that you go to the home page of that website to determine if it is still available or has moved to a new webpage or website.

If you go to the website and can't find it on your own, use the *Contact Us* information that most websites have to get help finding it. Anyone can help, but the person maintaining the website, the Webmaster or Webminister, should be most knowledgeable about what has been added or taken off the website.

Another technique is to use your favorite search engine, such as Google or Yahoo!, and type in the title or key words. Since the Internet is dynamic and always changing, you might find the information in a new location, or you might even find newer information that what I have presented here.

The following list of Internet links is presented alphabetically, followed by the same links listed by subject. This list could be much longer, but I have chosen what I believe are the best websites for chaplaincy information and issues. Let me apologize for leaving anyone out, but please contact me to be included on future lists (jgraves@reachone.com). Almost every denomination has a chaplaincy page on their website and many countries have a variety of chaplaincy organizations.

In late 2006, a search of Google on the Internet for the word *chaplain* shows 9,310,000 webpages; *military chaplain* - 3,090,000 webpages; *hospital chaplain* - 2,060,000 webpages; *prison chaplain* - 1,370,000 webpages; *mental health chaplain* – 1,040,000 webpages. The numbers were a little higher by using the word *chaplaincy* instead of *chaplain*. Searching for *spiritual care* will bring up a different group of websites with a little redundancy.

# ALPHABETICAL LISTING OF LINKS

(Same links by subject below)


Airport Chapel Program, Chicago  www.airportchapels.org/

American Academy of Experts in Traumatic Stress www.aaets.org

American Association of Pastoral Counselors (AAPC) www.aapc.org

Americans for Better Care of the Dying www.abcd-caring.org/

American Hospice Foundation www.americanhospice.org/

Apostleship of the Sea (for Catholics, seagoing and certain ports) www.aos-usa.org

Assemblies of God Chaplaincy Program http://chaplaincy.ag.org/gen_requirements.cfm

Association for Clinical Pastoral Education (ACPE) www.acpe.edu

Association for Death Education and Counseling www.adec.org/

Association of Professional Chaplains (APC) www.professionalchaplains.org

Association of Theological Schools www.ats.edu

Aviation Chaplains, International members.iinet.com.au/~holloway1/index.html

Benson-Henry Institute for Mind Body Medicine www.mbmi.org

Buddhist Chaplaincy Training www.sfzc.org/news/content/view/215/43/ also
www.sati.org

Business and Industrial Chaplains www.nibic.com/

Canadian Association for Pastoral Practice and Education (CAPPE) www.cappe.org

Canadian Forces Chaplain Branch www.forces.gc.ca/chapgen/engraph/home_e.asp

Chaplains at Work www.chaplainsatwork.com

Charteris Foundation www.charteris.org (Support for police and fire chaplains in the Northwest)

Churches Council on Theological Education in Canada www.web.net/~ccte

Civil Air Patrol www.cap.org

Civil Aviation Apostolate, Catholic www.nccbuscc.org/mrs/pcmr/onmove/airport.shtml

Coalition On Ministry In Specialized Settings www.comissnetwork.org

College of Pastoral Supervision and Psychotherapy www.cpsp.org

Corporate Chaplains of America www.iamchap.org

Correctional Chaplains Assoc (prisons, jails) www.correctionalchaplains.org

Critical Incident Stress Management www.cismperspectives.com

Duke Institute on Care at the End of Life www.iceol.duke.edu/

Duke University Center for Spirituality, Theology, and Health www.dukespiritualityandhealth.org/

ELCA Chaplaincy www.elca.org/chaplains/mcpcce/mcpcce_committee.html

Episcopal Church Office for Armed Services, Healthcare and Prison Ministries www.ecusa.anglican.org/ashapm

European Network for Healthcare Chaplains www.eurochaplains.org

Federation of Fire Chaplains www.firechaplains.org

George Washington Institute for Spirituality and Health www.gwish.org.cnchost.com/index.htm

German Society for Pastoral Psychology www.pastoralpsychologie.de

Healthcare Chaplaincy www.healthcarechaplaincy.org

Hospice Association of America www.hospice-america.org/

Hospice Foundation of America www.hospicefoundation.org/

Hospital Chaplaincy Gateway www.hospitalchaplain.com

Hospital Chaplains of America www.hcmachaplains.org

Independent Fundamental Churches of America www.ifca.org

International Association for Hospice & Palliative Care www.hospicecare.com/

International Center for the Integration of Health and Spirituality www.nihr.org/

International Chaplains Association www.christianchaplain.org

International Christian Maritime Association www.icma.as/

International Conference of Police Chaplains www.icpc4cops.org

International Conference of Police Chaplains, Northwest www.icpcnw.org

International Counsel on Pastoral Care & Counselling www.icpcc.net

International Critical Incident Stress Foundation www.icisf.org/

International Fellowship of Chaplains www.ifoc.org

International Fellowship of Hospice Chaplains www.ifoc.org/ifhosc.htm

International Pastoral Care Network for Social Responsibility www.ipcnsr.org

Islamic Chaplaincy Program www.macdonald.hartsem.edu/chaplaincy/index.html

Jewish Hospice & Chaplaincy Network www.jewishhospice.com/

Jewish Welfare Board Jewish Chaplains Council http://www.jcca.org/jwb/

John Templeton Foundation www.templeton.org/

Journal of Pastoral Care Publications (JPC) www.jcpc.org

Kay Spiritual Life Center, American University, Washington D.C. Chaplaincy List www.american.edu/ocl/kay/chaplains.html

Lutheran Chaplaincy Service www.spiritualcare.org

Lutheran Association for Maritime Ministry www.lutheranmaritimeworld.net

Marketplace Ministries www.marketplaceministries.com

Mental Health Chaplaincy www.mentalhealthchaplain.org

Military Chaplains Association www.mca-usa.org/home.htm

Mission to Seafarers  www.missiontoseafarers.org/

National Association of Catholic Chaplains USA (NACC) www.nacc.org

National Association of Jewish Chaplains www.najc.org

National Center for Crisis Management www.nc-cm.org

National Hospice and Palliative Care Organization www.nhpco.org/

National Hospice Organization www.nhpco.org

National Institute of Business and Industrial Chaplains www.nibic.com

National Institute for Jewish Hospice www.nijh.org/

National Prison Hospice Association www.npha.org/

National VA Chaplain Center www.chaplain.med.va.gov/Chaplain/

New York Board of Rabbis (Chaplaincy Program) www.nybr.org/

North American Maritime Ministry Association www.namma.org/

Pastoral Care Week www.pastoralcareweek.org

Pediatric Chaplains www.pediatricchaplains.org

Pennsylvania Society of Chaplains www.societyofchaplains.org/

Practice of Ministry in Canada Magazine www.pmcmagazine.com

Religious Tolerance www.religioustolerance.org

Robert Wood Johnson Foundation www.rwjf.org/

Royal Army (British & Irish) Chaplains' Department
www.army.mod.uk/chaps/index.htm

Society for Intercultural Pastoral Care & Counselling www.sipcc.org

Spiritual Direction www.sdiworld.org

Spiritual Leadership www.executivesoul.com

Spirituality and Health www.spiritualityhealth.com/

United Church of Christ www.chhsm.org/members/pcc.html

United Full Gospel National Chaplains Association www.biblical-life.com/nca/index.htm

United Methodist Section of Chaplains and Related Ministries www.gbhem.org

University of Minnesota, Center for Spirituality and Healing www.csh.umn.edu/

U.S. Air Force Chaplain Services www.usafhc.af.mil

U.S. Air Force Academy Chapel www.usafa.af.mil/superintendent/hc/

U.S. Army Chaplaincy www.usarmychaplain.com

U.S. Army Chaplain School www.usachcs.army.mil/

U.S. Coast Guard www.uscg.mil/hq/chaplain/index.htm

U.S. Merchant Marine Academy, Office of the Chaplain
www.usmma.edu/about/marinerschapel/staff.htm

U.S. Military Academy, West Point www.usma.edu/Chaplain/index.htm

U.S. Navy Chaplaincy www.chaplain.navy.mil

U.S. Naval Academy Chaplain www.usna.edu/Chaplains/

Workplace Chaplains in Scotland www.scim.org/

# LINKS BY SUBJECT

Civil Aviation/Airport, Corrections/Prisons/Jails, Countries, Counseling,

Critical Incident/Red Cross, Cruise Ships/Maritime/Ports, Faith Groups,

General Chaplaincy, General Education, Homeless, Hospital, Hospice,

Mental Health, Military, Police/Fire/Emergency,

Spirituality and Health, Workplace/Business/Corporate/Industrial

## CIVIL AVIATION & AIRPORT

Catholic Civil Aviation Apostolate  www.nccbuscc.org/mrs/pcmr/onmove/airport.shtml

Airport Chapel Programs (There are many, and these two are representative).
Chicago Airport Chapel Program  www.airportchapels.org/

City of Phoenix Airport Chapel Program, Sky Harbor Interfaith Chaplaincy,
http://phoenix.gov/AVIATION/travel_assist/chaplaincy.html

International Aviation Chaplains  Personal website of Rev. Holloway
http://members.iinet.com.au/~holloway1/index.html

Vatican Guidance for Catholic Aviation Chaplains
www.vatican.va/roman_curia/pontifical_councils/migrants/s_index_civilaviation/rc_pc_
migrants_sectioncivilaviation.htm

## CORRECTIONS, PRISONS, JAILS

Correctional Chaplains Assoc (prisons, jails) www.correctionalchaplains.org

Episcopal Church Office for Armed Services, Healthcare and Prison Ministries
www.ecusa.anglican.org/ashapm

National Prison Hospice Association www.npha.org/

# COUNTRIES

## Canada

Practice of Ministry in Canada Magazine www.pmcmagazine.com

Churches Council on Theological Education in Canada www.web.net/~ccte

## Britain & Ireland

Royal Army (British & Irish) Chaplains' Department
www.army.mod.uk/chaps/index.htm

## Europe

European Network for Healthcare Chaplains www.eurochaplains.org

European Counsel on Pastoral Care & Counselling www.ecpcc.info

International Counsel on Pastoral Care & Counselling www.icpcc.net

Society for Intercultural Pastoral Care & Counselling www.sipcc.org

International Pastoral Care Network for Social Responsibility www.ipcnsr-peace.org

## German

German Society for Pastoral Psychology www.pastoralpsychologie.de

## Scotland

Workplace Chaplains in Scotland www.scim.org/

# COUNSELING

American Association of Pastoral Counselors (AAPC) www.aapc.org

College of Pastoral Supervision and Psychotherapy www.cpsp.org

European Counsel on Pastoral Care & Counselling www.ecpcc.info

German Society for Pastoral Psychology www.pastoralpsychologie.de

Journal of Pastoral Care Publications www.jcpc.org

International Counsel on Pastoral Care & Counselling www.icpcc.net

Society for Intercultural Pastoral Care & Counselling www.sipcc.org


## CRITICAL INCIDENT, RED CROSS

American Academy of Experts in Traumatic Stress www.aaets.org, offers board certification as a crisis chaplain, and has a resource center for stresses of all kinds, i.e. adoption stress, date rape, university and school stress, books, audio tapes, library, disaster response, and more.

American Red Cross. Go to the website of your local American Red Cross chapter (or www.redcross.org, which will direct you to your local Red Cross chapter) and tell them you are interested in their Disaster Relief program and being a volunteer member of the Spiritual Care Team. They also have the Air Incident Response Team, and the Disaster Mortuary Operational Response Team.

Critical Incident Stress Management www.cismperspectives.com/

International Critical Incident Chaplaincy
www.icisf.org/about/faculty/instructors.asp?id=39

National Center for Crisis Management www.nc-cm.org


## CRUISE SHIPS, MARITIME & PORTS

Apostleship of the Sea (for Catholics, seagoing and certain ports) www.aos-usa.org

International Christian Maritime Association www.icma.as/

Lutheran Association for Maritime Ministry (but open to all), Pastoral care for seafarers and fishermen www.lutheranmaritimeworld.net/

Mission to Seafarers www.missiontoseafarers.org/

North American Maritime Ministry Association www.namma.org/. Actually an international ministry, which includes ministry to ships anchored off shore, port chapels, training, and travel opportunities.

U.S. Merchant Marine Academy, Office of the Chaplain
www.usmma.edu/about/marinerschapel/staff.htm

CRUISE SHIPS

If you are interested in a taking an all-expense paid cruise as a chaplain, contact the following organizations below. Sometimes it can be a little daunting finding the right information, and I would suggest calling them directly. Some will put you in touch with a preferred travel agent.

Carnival Cruise Lines www.Carnival.com, then click on *Fun Jobs*

Celebrity Cruise Lines www.celebritycruises.com

Disney Cruise Lines http://disneycruise.disney.go.com

Royal Caribbean Cruise Lines www.royalcaribbean.com

Norwegian Cruise Lines www.ncl.com

Princess Cruise Lines www.princes.com


EDUCATION
(Almost all websites have education information,
but these talk about education in general)

Association for Clinical Pastoral Education (ACPE) www.acpe.edu

Association for Death Education and Counseling www.adec.org/

Association of Professional Chaplains (APC) www.professionalchaplains.org

Association of Theological Schools www.ats.edu

Buddhist Chaplaincy Training www.sfzc.org/news/content/view/215/43/ also www.sati.org

Canadian Association for Pastoral Practice and Education (CAPPE) www.cappe.org

Churches Council on Theological Education in Canada www.web.net/~ccte

Critical Incident Stress Management www.cismperspectives.com

National Association of Catholic Chaplains USA (NACC) www.nacc.org

National Association of Jewish Chaplains www.najc.org

National Center for Crisis Management www.nc-cm.org

# EMPLOYMENT

Comprehensive list of job opportunity websites www.spirit-filled.org/chaplainpositions.htm#healthcare

Suggested key words for job searches: chaplain, spiritual, pastoral. Chaplain will also catch "chaplaincy," spiritual will also catch "spirituality." For leadership positions, also include "manager" and "mission", because some department heads are responsible for "mission services," which includes the hospital chaplaincy/spiritual care program.

# FAITH GROUPS

Assemblies of God  http://chaplaincy.ag.org/gen_requirements.cfm.\

Buddhist

Buddhist Information Web www.buddhistinformation.com/ This website has information on the major Buddhist sects.

Buddhist Chaplaincy Training www.sfzc.org/news/content/view/215/43/

Buddhist Studies www.sati.org;

Buddhist Prison Chaplaincy www.dharmalife.com/issue15/prisons.html

Catholic

Catholic Chaplains www.christianchaplains.org,

National Association of Catholic Chaplains www.nacc.org

Christian Reformed Church  www.crcna.org/pages/chaplaincy.cfm

Episcopalian  www.ecusa.anglican.org/ashapm

Independent Fundamental Churches of America ww.ifca.org

Jewish

Jewish Board of Rabbis of Southern California www.boardofrabbis.com (provide chaplains to area nursing homes and hospitals);

Jewish Chaplain Resources for Los Angeles Area www.jewishla.org/assets/applets/Jews_in_Hospitals_brochure-final_redo.pdf;

Jewish Hospice & Chaplaincy Network www.jewishhospice.com/

Jewish Welfare Board-Jewish Chaplains Council  www.jcca.org/jwb/;

National Association of Jewish Chaplains www.najc.org,

National Institute for Jewish Hospice www.nijh.org/

New York Board of Rabbis, Chaplaincy Program www.nybr.org/;

Lutheran

Chaplaincy Service  www.spiritualcare.org

ELCA Chaplaincy www.elca.org/chaplains/mcpcce/mcpcce_committee.html

Lutheran Association of Maritime Ministry www.lutheranmaritimeworld.net

Muslim

Islamic Chaplaincy Program www.macdonald.hartsem.edu/chaplaincy/index.html

Islamic Society of North America www.isna.net

United Church of Christ www.chhsm.org/members/pcc.html

United Full Gospel Churches  www.biblical-life.com/nca/index.htm

United Methodist Chaplains  www.gbhem.org


## GENERAL CHAPLAINCY ORGANIZATIONS

Coalition On Ministry In Specialized Settings www.comissnetwork.org

International Chaplains Association www.christianchaplains.org

International Fellowship of Chaplains www.ifoc.org

Pastoral Care Week www.pastoralcareweek.org

Pennsylvania Society of Chaplains www.societyofchaplains.org

## HOMELESS

Mental Health Chaplains www.mentalhealthchaplain.org

North American Association of Christian Social Work www.nacsw.org/index.shtml

There are many websites for homelessness and chaplaincy, which are part of larger ministries. Church and secular organizations work to provide homes for the homeless, social services, meals, street ministries, and many other services and ministries. If you are interested in chaplaincy to the homeless, peruse the different websites for opportunities in your local area.

## HOSPITAL

Association for Clinical Pastoral Education, Inc.(ACPE) www.acpe.edu

Association of Professional Chaplains (APC) www.professionalchaplains.org

Canadian Association for Pastoral Practice and Education (CAPPE) www.cappe.org

Episcopal Church Office for Armed Services, Healthcare and Prison Ministries www.ecusa.anglican.org/ashapm

European Network for Healthcare Chaplains www.eurochaplain.org

Healthcare Chaplaincy www.healthcarechaplaincy.org

Hospital Chaplaincy Gateway www.hospitalchaplain.com

Hospital Chaplains of America www.hcmachaplains.org

International Pastoral Care Network for Social Responsibility www.ipcnsr.org

National VA Chaplain Center www.chaplain.med.va.gov/Chaplain/

Pediatric Chaplains www.pediatricchaplains.org

## HOSPICE

Americans for Better Care of the Dying www.abcd-caring.org/

American Hospice Foundation www.americanhospice.org/

Association for Clinical Pastoral Education, Inc.(ACPE) www.acpe.edu

Association for Death Education and Counseling www.adec.org/

Association of Professional Chaplains (APC) www.professionalchaplains.org

Canadian Association for Pastoral Practice and Education (CAPPE) www.cappe.org

Duke Institute of Care at the End of Life www.iceol.duke.edu

Hospice Association of America www.hospice-america.org/

Hospice House, Tacoma www.fhshealth.org/services/hosp_house.asp

Hospice Foundation of America www.hospicefoundation.org/

International Association for Hospice & Palliative Care www.hospicecare.com/

International Fellowship of Hospice Chaplains www.ifoc.org/ifhosc.htm

Jewish Hospice & Chaplaincy Network www.jewishhospice.com/

National Hospice and Palliative Care Organization www.nhpco.org/

National Hospice Organization www.nhpco.org

National Institute for Jewish Hospice www.nijh.org/

National Prison Hospice Association www.npha.org


MENTAL HEALTH

Episcopal Mental Illness Network www.eminnews.org/

International Pastoral Care Network for Social Responsibility www.ipcnsr.org

Mental Health Chaplaincy www.mentalhealthchaplain.org

National Alliance for the Mentally Ill
www.nami.org/MSTemplate.cfm?Section=FaithNet_NAMI1&Site=FaithNet_NAMI&Te
mplate=/MSTemplate.cfm?Section=FaithNet_NAMI1&Site=FaithNet_NAMI&Template
=/TaggedPage/TaggedPageDisplay.cfm&TPLID=66&ContentID=33925&micrositeID=1
76

North American Association of Christian Social Work www.nacsw.org/index.shtml

Pathways to Promise (Resources) www.pathways2promise.org/

Pierce County, Washington www.associatedministries.org/pages/MHC.htm

Presbyterian Serious Mental Illness Network www.pcusa.org/phewa/psmin.htm

United Church of Christ, Mental Illness Network www.min-ucc.org/


MILITARY

Canadian Forces Chaplain Branch www.forces.gc.ca/chapgen/engraph/home_e.asp

Civil Air Patrol www.cap.org

Episcopal Church Office for Armed Services, Healthcare
and Prison Ministries www.ecusa.anglican.org/ashapm

Military Chaplains Association www.mca-usa.org/home.htm

National VA Chaplain Center www.chaplain.med.va.gov/Chaplain/

Royal Army (British & Irish) Chaplains' Department
www.army.mod.uk/chaps/index.htm

U.S. Air Force Chaplain Services Homepage www.usafhc.af.mil

U.S. Air Force Academy Chapel www.usafa.af.mil/superintendent/hc/

U.S. Army Chaplaincy Homepage www.usarmychaplain.com

U.S. Army Chaplain School www.usachcs.army.mil/

U.S. Coast Guard www.uscg.mil/hq/chaplain/index.htm

U.S. Merchant Marine Academy, Office of the Chaplain
www.usmma.edu/about/marinerschapel/staff.htm

U.S. Military Academy, West Point www.usma.edu/Chaplain/index.htm

U.S. Navy Chaplaincy Corps Homepage www.chaplain.navy.mil

U.S. Navy Academy Chaplain www.usna.edu/Chaplains/

POLICE, FIRE, EMERGENCY

Police

International Conference of Police Chaplains www.icpc4cops.org

International Conference of Police Chaplains, Northwest www.icpcnw.org

International Critical Incident Stress Foundation www.icisf.org/

International Fellowship of Chaplains www.ifoc.org

Police & Fire

Charteris Foundation www.charteris.org (Support for police and fire chaplains in the Northwest)

International Fellowship of Chaplains www.ifoc.org

Fire & Emergency

Federation of Fire Chaplains www.firechaplains.org

International Fellowship of Chaplains www.ifoc.org

International Critical Incident Stress Foundation www.icisf.org/

SPIRITUALITY AND HEALTH

Benson-Henry Institute for Mind Body Medicine www.mbmi.org

Duke University Center for Spirituality, Theology, and Health
www.dukespiritualityand health.org

George Washington Institute for Spirituality and Health
www.gwish.org.cnchost.com/index.htm

International Center for the Integration of Health and Spirituality www.nihr.org

John Templeton Foundation www.templeton.org

Kay Spiritual Life Center, American University, Washington D.C. Chaplaincy List
www.american.edu/ocl/kay/chaplains.html

Religious Tolerance www.religioustolerance.org

Robert Wood Johnson Foundation www.rwjf.org

Spiritual Direction www.sdiworld.org

Spirituality and Health www.spiritualityhealth.com

Spiritual Leadership www.executivesoul.com

University of Minnesota, Center for Spirituality and Health www.csh.umn.edu

## WORKPLACE, BUSINESS, CORPORATE, INDUSTRIAL

Business and Industrial Chaplains www.nibic.com/

Chaplains at Work www.chaplainsatwork.com

Corporate Chaplains of America www.iamchap.org

Marketplace Ministries www.marketplaceministries.com

National Institute of Business and Industrial Chaplains www.nibic.com

Spiritual Leadership www.executivesoul.com

Workplace Chaplains in Scotland www.scim.org/

| **MEDICAL INDICATIONS** | **PATIENT PREFERENCES** |
|---|---|
| The Principles of Beneficence (Maximize Benefit) and Nonmaleficence (Avoid Harm) | The Principle of Respect for Autonomy |
| 1. What is the patient's medical problem? history? diagnosis? Prognosis? | 1. Is the patient mentally capable and legally competent? Is there evidence of incapacity? |
| 2. Is the problem acute? chronic? critical? emergent? reversible? | 2. If competent, what is the patient stating about preferences for treatment? |
| 3. What are the goals of treatment? (Restoration of health; relief of symptoms; restoration of impaired function; saving life; preventing untimely death; assisting in a peaceful death). Given all the possibilities, what is the goal for this patient? | 3. Has the patient been informed of benefits and risks, understood this information, and given consent? |
| 4. What are the plans in case of therapeutic failure? | 4. If incapacitated, who is the appropriate surrogate? Is the surrogate using appropriate standards for decision-making? |
| 5. In sum, how can this patient be benefited by medical and nursing care, and how can harm be avoided? | 5. Has the patient expressed prior preferences, e.g. Advance Directive, Do Not Resuscitate (DNR), Living Will. |
| Other questions: 1. What are we accomplishing? | 6. Is the patient unwilling or unable to cooperate with medical treatment? if so, why? |
| 2. Is the expected outcome worth the effort? | 7. In sum, is the patient's rights to choose being respected to the extent possible in ethics and law? |
| 3. Do the benefits justify the risks? | |
| **QUALITY OF LIFE** | **CONTEXTUAL FEATURES** |
| The Principles of Beneficence, Nonmaleficence, and Respect for Autonomy | The Principles of Loyalty, Fairness, and Justice |
| 1. What are the prospects, with or without treatment, for a return to normal life? | 1. Are there family issues that might influence treatment decisions? |
| 2. What physical, mental, and social deficits is the patient likely to experience if treatment succeeds? | 2. Are there provider (physicians and nurses) issues that might influence treatment decisions? |
| 3. Are there biases that might prejudice the provider's evaluation of the patient's quality of life? | 3. Are there financial and economic factors? |
| 4. Is the patient's present or future condition such that their continued life might be judged undesirable? | 4. Are there religious or cultural factors? |
| 5. Is there any plan and rationale to forgo treatment? | 5. Are there limits on confidentiality? |
| 6. Are there plans for comfort and palliative care? | 6. Are there problems of allocation of resources? |
| | 7. How does the law affect treatment decisions? |
| | 8. Is clinical research or teaching involved? |
| | 9. Is there any conflict of interest on the part of the providers or the institution? |

---

[242] Jonsen, *Clinical Ethics*, 11.

# APPENDIX C – INTRODUCTION TO CHAPLAINCY COURSE OUTLINE

## INTRODUCTION TO CHAPLAINCY

### Suggested Course Outline for 5-Day Module

### DAY 1

Historical Review of Chaplaincy in the Bible, Military, and Hospitals.

Lecture and discussion on the following topics:

1. The Bible and the role of clergy in chaplaincy-like settings.

2. Origin of the chaplain name: Martin of Tours.

3. Patron saint of chaplaincy : St. John Capistrano.

3. Military chaplaincy from ancient times to present.

4. Origins of hospital chaplaincy.

5. Modern chaplaincy.

6. Female chaplaincy.

7. Chaplaincy leadership issues.

### DAY 2

Different Chaplaincies, Education, Certification, Requirements, Expectations, Attitudes, and Employment.

Lecture and discussion on the following topics:

1. Different Chaplaincies.

2. Education Requirements, Certification, Requirements of Different Chaplaincies.

3. The role of JCAHO, why it is important, and how it affects chaplaincy.

4. Certification Agencies: APC, NACC.

5. Education Opportunities: CPE, Counseling.

6. Expectations: Expectations of the chaplain candidate, expectations of the hiring agency, expectations of the agency seeking a volunteer chaplain.

7. Attitudes - discussion of compromise, restrictions, freedoms, challenges.

8. Discussion of chaplaincy links.

9. Employment opportunities: part-time, per diem, full-time.


DAY 3

Explore Calling, Self-Examination, Pastoral Theology of Chaplaincy, Spirituality.

Lecture and discussion on the following topics:

1. What is a "calling?" How does it work? What might be some indications of a calling to chaplaincy? Is a response necessary? How do we respond?

2. How do we examine ourselves?

3. What is pastoral theology? How do we develop a pastoral theology for our ministry?

4. What is Spirituality? What is Spiritual Assessment? Where does it take place? How is it done? Developing own Spiritual Assessment model.

5. Study and discussion of *The Wounded Healer* concept (book read before class).

DAY 4

Guest Speaker (local chaplain – at least one, no more than two), Counseling Techniques,

Disenfranchised Grief, Theological Reflection.

Lecture and discussion on the following topics:

1. Crisis and Trauma Counseling, CISM (classroom practicum)

2. Disenfranchised Grief.

3. Medical Ethics.

4. Theological Reflection (what it is, how it is done).

5. Self-Care (What it is, why it is important, how it is done).


DAY 5

Visit local chaplain ministry.

1. Meet with the leadership and chaplain(s) to discuss their ministry (history, people

needs, ministry needs, how the chaplain does ministry; challenges, strengths, weaknesses,

growing edges; leadership and management issues; growth issues; the future.).

2. Tour organization.

3. Retire to a meeting room to discuss the tour, final questions, follow-up, and completion

of class/instructor feedback form.

# OTHER POSSIBLE CHAPLAIN COURSES

Advance courses particular to chaplains include some or all of the following:

Counseling Series

    Bereavement

    Conflict Resolution

    Critical Incident Training: domestic violence, homicide, suicide, natural disasters

    Domestic Abuse

    Loss and Grief

    Mental Illness

    Substance Abuse and Alcoholism

    Trauma and Crisis Counseling

    Verbal and Non-Verbal Communication

Cultural Diversity and Inclusiveness

    Toleration and Openness in Religion

Leadership for Chaplains

Medical Ethics

Self-Care for Ministry

Thanatology

    Death and Dying

    Hospice Ministry

    Death and Afterlife in Different Religions

Working with Volunteers, Assistants, and Aides

Worship Practicum

Creating and leading services and sacraments while being sensitive to the differences of denominations and faith groups, and in various settings (outside, bedside, aboard ship, a small chapel, small spaces, mobility and logistical issues, various music options, with volunteers.).

# BIBLIOGRAPHY

Ackermann, Henry F. *He Was Always There: The United States Army Chaplain Ministry in the Vietnam Conflict*. Washington, DC: Office of the Chief of Chaplains, Department of the Army, 1989.

Almedingen, E.M. *St. Francis of Assisi: A great life in brief*. New York: Barnes & Noble Books, 1967.

Blackaby, Henry T., and Richard Blackaby. *Spiritual Leadership: Moving people on to God's agenda*. Nashville: Broadman & Holman, 2001.

Bonem, Mike, and Roger Patterson. *Leading from the Second Chair: Serving your church, fulfilling your role, and realizing your dreams*. San Francisco: Jossey-Bass, 2005.

Bonhoeffer, Dietrich. *Life Together*. New York: HarperCollins, 1954.

Bonhoeffer, Dietrich. *The Cost of Discipleship*. New York: Macmillan, 1959.

Brinsfield, John W. Jr. *Encouraging Faith, Supporting Soldiers: A History of the United States Army Chaplain Corps, 1975-1995*. 6 vols. Washington, DC: Office of the Chief of Chaplains, Department of the Army, 1998.

Brinsfield, John W. Jr., Williams C. Davis, Benedict Maryniak, James I. Robertson, Jr. *Faith in the Fight–Civil War Chaplains*. Mechanicsburg, PA: Stackpole Books, 2003.

Brinsfield, John W. Jr., ed. *The Spirit Divided–Memoirs of Civil War Chaplains–The Confederacy*. Macon, GA: Mercer University Press, 2005.

Burton, Laurel Arthur, ed. *Making Chaplaincy Work: Practical approaches*. New York: Haworth Press, 1988.

Callanan, Maggie, and Patricia Kelley. *Final Gifts: Understanding the Special Awareness, Needs, and Communications of the Dying*. New York: Bantam Books, 1997.

Carr, Charles A. *"Revisiting the Concept of Disenfranchised Grief."* Pages 41-42 in *Disenfranchised Grief: New directions, challenges, and strategies for practice*. Edited by Kenneth J. Doka, Champaign, Ill.: Research Press, 2002.

Cash, Carey H. *A Table in the Presence*. Nashville: W Publishing, 2004.

Cedar, Paul. *A Life of Prayer: Cultivating the inner life of the Christian leader.* Nashville: Word Publishing, 1998.

Clinebell, Howard, *Basic Types of Pastoral Care and Counseling–Resources for the ministry of healing and growth.* Nashville: Abingdon, 1984.

Clinton, J. Robert. *The Making of a Leader: Recognizing the lessons and stages of leadership development.* Colorado Springs: NavPress, 1988.

Dass, Ram, and Paul Gorman. *How Can I Help? Stories and reflections on service.* New York: Alfred A. Knopt, 1987.

Deep, Sam Lyle Sussman. *Smart Moves for People in Charge.* New York: Addison-Wesley, 1995.

Dickens, William E., Jr. *Answering the Call: The Story of the US Military Chaplaincy from the Revolution through the Civil War.* Printed copy of dissertation in book form from dissertation.com, 1998.

Doka, Kenneth J., ed. *Disenfranchised Grief: New directions, challenges, and strategies for practice.* Champaign: Research Press, 2002.

Fichter, Joseph Henry. *Religion and Pain: The spiritual dimensions of health care.* New York: Crossroad, 1981.

Geisler, Norman L. *Christian Ethics: Options and Issues.* Grand Rapids: Baker Book House, 1989.

Gire, Ken. *Seeing What is Sacred: Becoming more spiritually sensitive to the everyday moments of life.* Nashville: W Publishing Group, 2006.

Gire, Ken. *The North Face of God: Hope for times when God seems indifferent.* Colorado Springs: Alive Communications, 2005.

Gushwa, Robert L. *The Best and Worst of Times: The United States Army Chaplaincy, 1920-1945.* 6 vols. Washington, DC: Office of the Chief of Chaplains, Department of the Army, 1977.

Haugk, Kenneth C. *Don't Sing Songs to a Heavy Heart: How to relate to those who are suffering.* St Louis: Stephen Ministries, 2004.

Hemenway, Joan E. *Inside the Circle: A historical and practical inquiry concerning process groups in clinical pastoral education.* Decatur, GA: Journal of Pastoral Care Publications, 1996.

Herrington, Jim, R. Robert Creech, and Trisha Taylor. *The Leader's Journey: Accepting the call to personal and congregational transformation.* San Francisco: Jossey-Bass, 2003.

Hillman, James. *In Search: Psychology and Religion* 3 ed. Woodstock, CT: Spring Publications, 1994.

Hybels, Bill. *Courageous Leadership.* Grand Rapids: Zondervan, 2002.

Johnson, Christopher, and Marsha G. McGee. *How Different Religions View Death and Afterlife* 2 ed. Philadelphia: The Charles Press, 1998.

Joiner, Reggie, Lane Jones, and Andy Stanley. *The 7 Practices of Effective Ministry.* Sisters, OR: Multnomah, 2004.

Jonsen, Albert R, Mark Siegler, William J. Winslade. *Clinical Ethics: A practical approach to ethical decisions in clinical medicine.* 6 ed. New York: McGraw-Hill, 2006.

Killen, Patricia O'Connell and John de Beer. *The Art of Theological Reflection.* New York: Crossroad, 1998.

Koenig, Harold G. *Spirituality in Patient Care: Why, how, when, and what.* Philadelphia: Templeton Foundation Press, 2002.

Kübler-Ross, Elisabeth. *On Death and Dying: What the dying have to teach doctors, nurses, clergy, and their own families.* New York: Scribner, 1969.

Kübler-Ross, Elisabeth. *Questions & Answers on Death and Dying: A companion volume to On Death and Dying.* New York: Touchstone, 1974.

Kübler-Ross, Elisabeth. *Death: The Final Stage of Growth.* Englewood Cliffs, NJ: Prentice-Hall, 1975.

Lawson, Kenneth E. *Faith and Hope in a War-Torn Land: The US Army Chaplaincy in the Balkans, 1995-2005.* Fort Leavenworth: Combat Studies Institute Press, 2006.

Mack, Ronald, Sr. *The Basics of Hospital Chaplaincy.* Longwood, FL: Xulon Press, 2003.

Maxwell, John C. *Developing the Leader Within You.* Nashville: Thomas Nelson, 1993.

McBride, J. LeBron. *Spiritual Crisis: Surviving trauma to the soul.* Binghamton: Haworth, 1998.

McNeal, Reggie. *Practicing Greatness: 7 principles of extraordinary spiritual leaders.* San Francisco: Jossey-Bass, 2006.

217

Mitchell, Kenneth R. *Hospital Chaplain.* Philadelphia: Westminster, 1972.

Moore, Thomas. *The Soul's Religion.* New York: HarperCollins, 2002.

Morris, Virginia. *Talking About Death.* Chapel Hill, NC: Algonquin Books, 2001.

Muller, Wayne. *How Then Shall We Live? Four simple questions that reveal the beauty and meaning of our lives.* New York: Bantam Books, 1997.

Muller, Wayne. *Sabbath: Finding rest, renewal, and delight in our busy lives.* New York: Bantam Books, 1999.

Norton, Herman A. *Struggling for Recognition: The United States Army Chaplaincy, 1791-1865.* 6 vols. Washington, DC: Office of the Chief of Chaplains, Department of the Army, 1977.

Nouwen, Henri J. M. *The Wounded Healer.* New York: Doubleday, 1972.

Oxford American Dictionary-Heald Colleges Edition. New York: Avon Books, 1982.

Pence, Gregory E. *Classic Cases in Medical Ethics: Accounts of cases that have shaped medical ethics, with philosophical, legal, and historical backgrounds.* New York: McGraw Hill, 1990.

Pruyser, Paul W. *The Minister as Diagnostician: Personal problems in pastoral perspective.* Louisville: Westminster John Knox, 1976.

Sanders, J. Oswald. *Spiritual Leadership: Principles of excellence for every believer.* Chicago: Moody, 1994.

Stone, Howard W. *Crisis Counseling.* Minneapolis: Fortress, 1993.

Stover, Earl F. *Up From Handyman: The United States Army Chaplaincy, 1920-1945.* 6 vols. Washington, DC: Office of the Chief of Chaplains, Department of the Army, 1977.

Thompson, Parker C. *From Its European Antecedents to 1791: The United States Army Chaplaincy.* 6 vols. Washington, DC: Office of the Chief of Chaplain, Department of the Army, 1978.

Venzke, Rodger R. *Confidence in Battle, Inspiration in Peace: The United States Army Chaplaincy. 1945-1975,* 6 vols. Washington, DC: Office of the Chief of Chaplains, Department of the Army, 1977.

Wilson, Paul. *The Calm Technique: Meditation without magic or mysticism.* New York: Barnes & Noble Books, 1985.

Woolfe, Lorin. *Leadership Secrets from the Bible: From Moses to Matthew-Management Lessons for Contemporary Leaders*. New York: MJF Books, 2002.


## INTERNET PUBLICATIONS

Antiochian Orthodox Christian Archdiocese of North America. "Guidelines for Antiochian Orthodox Priests Serving as Chaplains and Clergy, and Laity Serving as Pastoral Counselors." *Antiochian Web.* http://www.antiochian.org/chaplain/pastoralcounselors (15 Nov 2006).

Assemblies of God USA. "Requirements." *Assemblies of God USA Web.* http://chaplaincy.ag.org/gen_requirements.cfm (7 Sep 2006).

Baker, Chris. "Airport Chaplain." 8 Jul 2005. *The Washington Times Web.* http://www.washtimes.com/business/20050707-104313-8780r.htm (4 Nov 2006).

Baker, Peter. "GOP Infighting on Detainees Intensifies Bush Threatens to Halt CIA Program if Congress Passes Rival Proposal." 2006. *Washington Post Web.* http://www.washingtonpost.com/wp-dyn/content/article/2006/09/15/AR2006091500483.html (16 Oct 2006).

Barna, George. "Unchurched." *The Barna Group Web.* http://www.barna.org/FlexPage.aspx?Page=Topic&TopicID=38 (12 Nov 2006).

Bishop, Donald M. "Six Chaplains, One Faith." Nov 2001 *The Embassy of the United States of America in Nigeria Web.* http://abuja.usembassy.gov/wwwhxrdnov10.html (14 Nov 2006).

Buddhist Information of North America. "What is Tibetan Buddhism?" *Buddhist Information Web.* http://www.buddhistinformation.com/tibetan/what_is_tibetan_buddhism.htm (17 Nov 2006).

Catholic Encyclopedia. "St. John Capistran." *Catholic Encyclopedia Web.* http://www.newadvent.org/cathen/08452.htm (30 Oct 2006).

Civil Air Patrol. "Info For Clergy." *Civil Air Patrol Web.* http://www.cap.org (10 Dec 2006).

Civil Air Patrol Chaplains' Service. "Senior Member Training Program Specialty Track Study Guide." Civil Air Patrol Publication 221 (E), 10 Jan 1995. *Civil Air Patrol Web.* http://level2.cap.gov/documents/u_082503085137.pdf (10 Dec 2006).

Congressional Research Service of the Library of Congress: Report to Congress. "House and Senate Chaplains." *U.S. Senate Web.* http://www.senate.gov/reference/resources/pdf/RS20427.pdf (22 Oct 2006).

Dana-Farber Medical Center. "Pastoral Care Staff." *Dana-Farber Medical Center Web.* http://www.dana-farber.org/pat/support/pastoral-care/chaplains.asp (7 Nov 2006).

Dictionary.com. "Decathect." (Based on the Random House Unabridged Dictionary, © Random House, Inc. 2006. Dictionary.com Unabridged v 1.0.1.). http://dictionary.reference.com/browse/decathect (3 Nov 2006).

Dictionary.com. "Sufferance." (Based on the American Heritage Dictionary of the English Language, 4 ed.). http://dictionary.reference.com/browse/sufferance (11 Nov 2006).

Donnelly, Doris. "Pilgrims and Tourists: Conflicting metaphors for the Christian journey to God." Spring 1992. *Spirituality Today Web.* http://www.spiritualitytoday.org/spir2day/92441donnelly.html (18 Nov 2006).

D'Souza, Alfred. "Happiness is a Journey." *Fleurdelis Web.* http://www.fleurdelis.com/happinessisajourney.htm (11 Nov 2006).

Duin, Julia. "Military chaplains told to shy from Jesus." 2005. *The Washington Times Web.* http://www.washtimes.com/national/20051221-121224-6972r.htm (22 Oct 2006).

Federation of Fire Department Chaplains. *Fire Chaplains Web.* http://www.firechaplains.org (12 Oct 2006).

Figen, Dorothy. "Is Buddhism a Religion?" *Buddhist Information Web.* http://www.buddhistinformation.com/is_buddhism_a_religion1.htm (17 Nov 2006).

Friedman, Gary. "Chaplaincy: Facing New and Old Challenges." http://www.correctionalchaplains.org/Garys%20Article/garytext.html (17 Oct 2006).

Genealogy Forum. "U.S. Civil War History & Genealogy Compiled References Regarding Black Confederates." *Genealogy Forum Web.* http://www.genealogyforum.com/gfaol/resource/Military/BlackConfederates.htm (10 Dec 2006).

International Conference of Police Chaplains. "Chaplains at Work." *ICPC4COPS.org.* http://www.icpc4cops.org/ (20 Oct 2006).

Jewish Women's Archive. "JWA Chaplain Bonnie Koppell." *Jewish Women's Archive Web.* http://www.jwa.org/discover/inthepast/infocus/military/chaplains/koppell.html (19 Oct 2006).

Joint Commission on the Accreditation of Healthcare Organizations. "About Us." Oct 2006. *JCAHO Web.* http://www.jointcommission.org/AboutUs/joint_commission_facts.htm (28 Oct 2006).

Longley, Robert. "Terror-Linked Group May Supply Muslim US Military Chaplains." 26 Sept 2003. *U.S. Government Info Web.* http://usgovinfo.about.com/b/a/029839.htm (15 Nov 2006).

Lorrain, Chuck. "Costs & Consequences: What is the price of full-time chaplaincy?" *International Conference of Police Chaplains Web.* http://www.icpc4cops.org/ (20 Oct 2006).

Lothene Experimental Archeology. "Women as Warriors-Celtic and Roman." *Lothene Web.* http://www.lothene.demon.co.uk/others/womenrom.html (28 Oct 2006).

McDonald, George. "Chapter XX: Robert Falconer." *Classic Reader Web.* http://classicreader.com/read.php/sid.1/bookid.1171/sec.58/ (11 Nov 2006).

MIT Student News. "Dharma in the Dorm: MIT Hires Buddhist Chaplain." *MIT Student Web.* http://www.stnews.org/rlr-823.htm (27 Sep 2006).

National Park Service. "The Braddock Campaign." *National Park Service Web.* http://www.nps.gov/fone/braddock.htm (27 Oct 2006).

Navy News. "First Armed Forces Buddhist Chaplain Commissioned." 22 Jul 2004. *Navy News Web.* http://www.news.navy.mil/search/display.asp?story_id=14387 (9 Nov 2006).

Office of the United Nations High Commissioner for Human Rights, Geneva, Switzerland. "Geneva Convention Relative to the Treatment of Prisoners of War." 2006. *Geneva Convention Web.* http://www.unhchr.ch/html/menu3/b/91.htm (9 Nov 2006).

Order of the Sisters of St. Francis of Philadelphia. "History." 2006. *Sisters of St Francis of Philadelphia Web.* http://www.osfphila.org/sp/about_us/history.html (21 Oct 2006).

Pickus, Abigail. "Jewish Chaplains Offer Spiritual Guidance." 1 Oct 1999. *Jewish News of Greater Phoenix Web.* http://www.jewishaz.com/jewishnews/991001/chaplain.shtml (14 Nov 2006).

Pope John Paul II. "Catholic Airport Chaplaincy in the 21st Century." 13 May 2003. *Vatican Web.* http://www.vatican.va/roman_curia/pontifical_councils/migrants/documents/rc_pc_migrants_doc_2003057_Aviation_Lyon_Marchetto_en.html (4 Nov 2006).

Religious Land Use and Institutionalized Persons Act. "Background." *RLUIPA.com.* http://www.rluipa.com/ (12 Oct 2006).

Religious Land Use and Institutionalized Persons Act. "Denial of Religious Materials Violates RLUIPA, First Amendment." *RLUIPA.com.* http://www.rluipa.com/index.php/topic/20.htm?PHPSESSID=de867d8e5d9ae142025a61 b8ac62e4d9 (12 Oct 2006).

Robinson, Harold L. "JWB Chaplains Bring Holiday to the Troops." *JWBCC Web.* http://www.jcca.org/jwb/ (16 Aug 2006).

Starcher, Keith. "Should You Hire a Workplace Chaplain?" 2003. *Christianity Today Web.* http://www.christianitytoday.com/workplace/articles/issue8-chaplain.html (10 Sept 2006).

Stuhlman, Daniel D. "Librarian's Lobby." Feb 2005. http://home.earthlink.net/~ddstuhlman/crc80.htm (14 Nov 2006).

Truman Presidential Museum and Library. "The Buck Stop." *Truman Library Web.* http://www.trumanlibrary.org/buckstop.htm (9 Nov 2006).

University of Queensland. "Chaplaincy Services." 26 May 2005. *University of Queensland Web.* http://www.uq.edu.au/hupp/index.html?page=25350&pid=25347 (16 Nov 2006).

University of Victoria. "Faith Groups and Interfaith Chaplains." 2006. *University of Victoria Web.* http://web.uvic.ca/interfaith/chaplains/ (18 Oct 2006).

Wikipedia Encyclopedia. "Transcendence." http://en.wikipedia.org/wiki/Transcendence (30 Nov 2006).

Wikipedia Encyclopedia. "Immanence." http://en.wikipedia.org/wiki/Immanence (30 Nov 2006).

Wikipedia Encyclopedia. "Terri Schiavo." http://www.en.wikipedia.org/wiki/Terri Schiavo (22 Oct 2006).

World Net Daily. "Faith Under Fire: Chaplain who prayed in Jesus' name convicted. Klingenschmitt jury now will consider punishment," 2006. *World Net Daily Web.* http://www.wnd.com/news/article.asp?ARTICLE_ID=51973 (23 Oct 2006).

Yale Center for Faith & Culture. "National Conference on Workplace Chaplaincy." 2006. *Yale University Web.* http://www.yale.edu/faith/esw/ncwc.htm (28 Sep 2006).


OTHER SOURCES

Association of Professional Chaplains. "Membership Offers Valuable Benefits." *Healing Spirit* 1 (2006): 34.

Clay, Annie. Buddhist Hospice and Hospital Chaplain. Interview 13 Nov 2006.

Hilsman, Gordon J. *Primary Spiritual Arenas.* Unpublished paper: Used by permission.

Head, Barbara. "The Transforming Power of Prison Hospice: Changing the Culture of Incarceration One Life at a Time." *Journal of Hospice & Palliative Nursing* 7 (2005): 354-9.

Krusemark, Mardi, Rev. Chaplain, Pediatric Grief and Loss Care Manager. Interview 14 Nov 2006.

Toolen, Tom. *Chaplains on Frontline in Corporate Wars.* The Spiritual Herald Newspaper. New York: Eastern Tsalagi Publishing Co (Aug 2004), 24.

Printed in the United Kingdom by
Lightning Source UK Ltd., Milton Keynes
141084UK00001B/91/A